MW01612592

FAITH

NEHEMIAH

&

WORK

HE READS TRUTH

HE READS TRUTH

EDITORIAL

EDITORS-IN-CHIEF
Raechel Myers and Amanda Bible Williams

CONTENT DIRECTOR
Russ Ramsey, MDiv., ThM.

MANAGING EDITOR
Jessica Lamb

EDITOR
Kara Gause

EDITORIAL ASSISTANT
Ellen Taylor

CREATIVE

CREATIVE DIRECTOR
Ryan Myers

ART DIRECTOR
Amanda Barnhart

DESIGNER
Kelsea Allen

PRODUCTION DESIGNER
Julie Allen

Photography used by permission.

@hereadstruth

hereadstruth.com

SUBSCRIPTION INQUIRIES
orders@hereadstruth.com

COLOPHON

This book was printed offset in Nashville, Tennessee, on 60# Lynx Opaque Text under the direction of He Reads Truth. The cover is 100# matte with a soft touch aqueous coating.

COPYRIGHT

ISBN 978-1-946282-66-8

Though the dates in this book have been carefully researched, scholars disagree on the dating of many biblical events.

Biblical site locations are estimates based on archaeological evidence and biblical scholarship.

Do you struggle with a sense of calling? Do you wonder what you should be doing with your life, and what role your faith plays in that equation? A short explanation about the ampersand in this book's title may help.

In writing credits for the Writers Guild of America, an ampersand is used to note that two writers worked alongside one another as a single voice. Using the word *and* to separate two names indicates the writers worked on the same project, but independently of one another. So while "written by Joel Coen & Ethan Coen" may appear to have the same meaning as "written by Joel Coen and Ethan Coen," the difference is actually quite significant.

Scripture shows us that our faith and our work should be joined by an ampersand. They work together, not independently of one another. Nehemiah gives us a great picture of this relationship. It is a book about work driven by faith.

Nehemiah is filled with the names of men and women who worked to rebuild the fallen walls and gates of Jerusalem. These people were doing work—hard work. Their names are included in this book, not for being celebrities or splitting the atom, but for moving rocks. Why does God's Holy Word contain a record of men and women stacking rocks? Because by faith they were doing the work God had called them to.

Maybe you wonder what work you've been called to. You wonder, *What should I be doing? Where should I invest my time?* Nehemiah tells us that many of these faithful workers focused on repairing the parts of the wall that were right outside their homes. They were doing the hard work that was in front of them. More often than not, this is our calling in life: to do the work that is in front of us, and to do it faithfully, for the glory of God.

As you study Nehemiah, think about the work to be done outside your own front door. Think about the relationship between what you believe and what you do with what you believe. What needs to be done? How can you help? Maybe that's your calling right now.

Read on,

RUSS RAMSEY
CONTENT DIRECTOR

"WE WANTED THE TYPEFACE TO FEEL HUMBLE AND HARD-WORKING, MUCH LIKE THE MEN IN THESE PHOTOS."

Nehemiah's focus on the relationship between faith and work provided us with the inspiration for our design choices in this Legacy Book.

The photography shows men at work, depicting a variety of workshops, tools, and workers in different occupations. We paired these modern images with a color palette drawn from WWII-era posters and workshop signs, choosing the dominant yellow of this book from paint swatches used for public service vehicles in the 1940s.

We wanted the typeface to feel humble and hardworking, much like the men in these photos. The main typeface, Gotham, is reminiscent of the no-nonsense, handcrafted signs prominent in cities and the technical lettering used by engineers and architects.

The notes grid you'll see on Saturdays and Sundays is inspired by the precision and clean lines of building plans. We also took this approach in designing the map on page 18, aiming to imitate the practical and functional appearance of a blueprint. "The Walls of Jerusalem" map, in particular, has an added function in its design. Unfold the map on the left, and leave it open as you read for a quick reference to the key places mentioned in Nehemiah.

For glory and beauty,

THE HE READS TRUTH CREATIVE TEAM

HOW TO USE THIS BOOK

Each book in the He Reads Truth Legacy Series™ provides space to read and study Scripture, make notes, and record prayers. As you build your library, you will have a record of your Bible-reading journey to reference and pass down.

3
WE PREPARED TO REBUILD THE WALLS

SCRIPTURE READING PLAN

This study book presents Nehemiah in daily readings, plus supplementary passages for additional context. The day titles offer a first-person summary of Nehemiah.

RESPONSE

Each daily reading includes wide margins for notes and prayers.

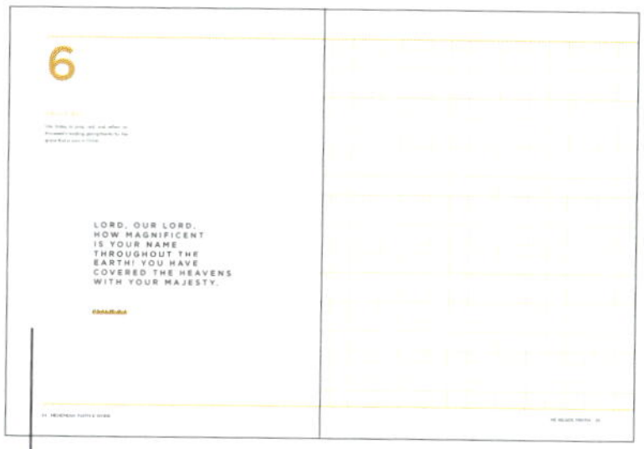
6
LORD, OUR LORD, HOW MAGNIFICENT IS YOUR NAME THROUGHOUT THE EARTH! YOU HAVE COVERED THE HEAVENS WITH YOUR MAJESTY.

GRACE DAY

Use Saturdays to pray, rest, and reflect on what you've read.

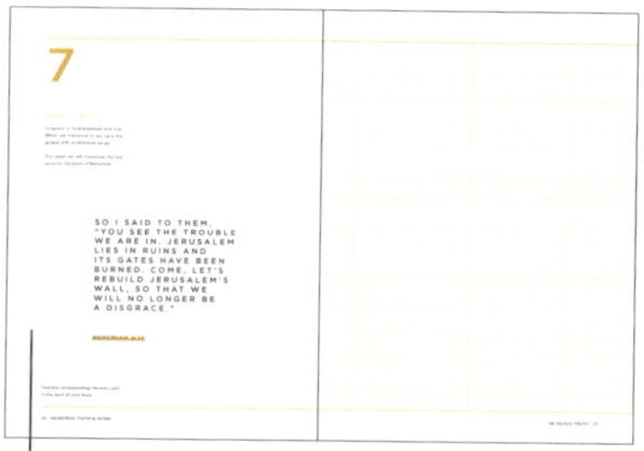
7
SO I SAID TO THEM, "YOU SEE THE TROUBLE WE ARE IN. JERUSALEM LIES IN RUINS AND ITS GATES HAVE BEEN BURNED. COME, LET'S REBUILD JERUSALEM'S WALL, SO THAT WE WILL NO LONGER BE A DISGRACE."

WEEKLY TRUTH

Sundays are set aside for weekly Scripture memorization.

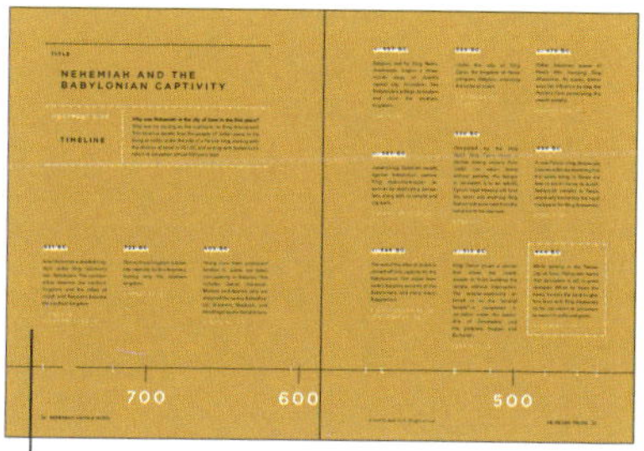
NEHEMIAH AND THE BABYLONIAN CAPTIVITY
TIMELINE
700
600
500

EXTRAS

This book features additional tools to help you gain a deeper understanding of the text.

For additional commentary on each day's reading, download the He Reads Truth™ app and choose the **Nehemiah** reading plan, or follow along at HeReadsTruth.com.

TABLE OF CONTENTS

EXTRAS

KEY VERSE

SO I SAID TO THEM, "YOU SEE THE TROUBLE WE ARE IN. JERUSALEM LIES IN RUINS AND ITS GATES HAVE BEEN BURNED. COME, LET'S REBUILD JERUSALEM'S WALL, SO THAT WE WILL NO LONGER BE A DISGRACE."

NEHEMIAH 2:17

ON THE TIMELINE:

Nehemiah was written in the late fifth century BC. Nehemiah's ministry in Jerusalem occurred in 444 BC, after he led the third major group of exiles back to Jerusalem. The Jewish people had been released by the decree of Cyrus in 538 BC and were allowed to return to Jerusalem at that time, though many remained in Babylon and Persia.

A LITTLE BACKGROUND:

Nehemiah was the cupbearer to the Persian king Artaxerxes I. Nehemiah returned to Jerusalem under a special leave of absence from the king and led the returned exiles in rebuilding the walls, resettling Jerusalem, and reestablishing the law of Moses in Israel.

The book of Nehemiah is written from the perspective of Nehemiah, though the author is never specifically named. This writing style in the Old Testament did not necessarily mean a work was autobiographical.

Until the third century AD, the books of Ezra and Nehemiah were regarded as a single text. Ezra is called a scribe in both Ezra and Nehemiah, and the oldest Jewish sources usually credit Ezra as the author of both texts.

MESSAGE & PURPOSE:

The book of Nehemiah records the rebuilding of the walls in Jerusalem despite opposition and difficulty. Nehemiah exhorts the people to remain faithful to the Lord and return to Him in the restored capital city of Israel. It is written to the people of Israel to remind them of God's redemptive plan; to encourage them to remain separate and pure in matters of doctrine, ethics, and customs; and to call them to remain steadfast in their covenant with God.

GIVE THANKS FOR THE BOOK OF NEHEMIAH:

The events which occurred in Nehemiah–the rebuilding of the walls, the stabilizing of Jerusalem, and the development of the Jewish community–all played key roles leading to the life and ministry of Jesus recorded in the Gospels. The rebuilt walls served the purpose of protecting a functional temple. The temple may not have been as magnificent as Solomon's temple, but it would serve as the central place of worship for the Jewish people for centuries until Christ removed the need for a physical temple.

1

MY PRAYER TO THE GOD OF HEAVEN

NEHEMIAH 1, DEUTERONOMY 30:1-5,
DEUTERONOMY 30:11-15, HEBREWS 7:25

NOTES

NEHEMIAH 1

[1] The words of Nehemiah son of Hacaliah:

News from Jerusalem

During the month of Chislev in the twentieth year, when I was in the fortress city of Susa, [2] Hanani, one of my brothers, arrived with men from Judah, and I questioned them about Jerusalem and the Jewish remnant that had survived the exile. [3] They said to me,

"THE REMNANT IN THE PROVINCE, WHO SURVIVED THE EXILE, ARE IN GREAT TROUBLE AND DISGRACE. JERUSALEM'S WALL HAS BEEN BROKEN DOWN, AND ITS GATES HAVE BEEN BURNED."

Nehemiah's Prayer

[4] When I heard these words, I sat down and wept. I mourned for a number of days, fasting and praying before the God of the heavens.
[5] I said,

> LORD, the God of the heavens, the great and awe-inspiring God who keeps his gracious covenant with those who love him and keep his
> commands, [6] let your eyes be open and your ears be attentive to hear your servant's prayer that I now pray to you day and night for your servants, the Israelites. I confess the sins we have committed against
> you. Both I and my father's family have sinned. [7] We have acted corruptly toward you and have not kept the commands, statutes, and
> ordinances you gave your servant Moses. [8] Please remember what you commanded your servant Moses: "If you are unfaithful, I will
> scatter you among the peoples. [9] But if you return to me and carefully observe my commands, even though your exiles were banished to the farthest horizon, I will gather them from there and bring them to the
> place where I chose to have my name dwell." [10] They are your servants and your people. You redeemed them by your great power and strong
> hand. [11] Please, Lord, let your ear be attentive to the prayer of your servant and to that of your servants who delight to revere your name. Give your servant success today, and grant him compassion in the presence of this man.

At the time, I was the king's cupbearer.

DEUTERONOMY 30:1-5, 11-15

NOTES

[1] “When all these things happen to you—the blessings and curses I have
set before you—and you come to your senses while you are in all the
nations where the LORD your God has driven you, [2] and you and your
children return to the LORD your God and obey him with all your heart
and all your soul by doing everything I am commanding you today,
[3] then he will restore your fortunes, have compassion on you, and gather
you again from all the peoples where the LORD your God has scattered
you. [4] Even if your exiles are at the farthest horizon, he will gather you
and bring you back from there. [5] The LORD your God will bring you into
the land your fathers possessed, and you will take possession of it. He will
cause you to prosper and multiply you more than he did your fathers.”

...

[11] “This command that I give you today is certainly not too difficult or
beyond your reach. [12] It is not in heaven so that you have to ask, ‘Who
will go up to heaven, get it for us, and proclaim it to us so that we may
follow it?’ [13] And it is not across the sea so that you have to ask, ‘Who
will cross the sea, get it for us, and proclaim it to us so that we may follow
it?’ [14] But the message is very near you, in your mouth and in your heart,
so that you may follow it. [15] See, today I have set before you life and
prosperity, death and adversity.”

HEBREWS 7:25

Therefore, he is able to save completely those who come to God through him, since he always lives to intercede for them.

2

THE KING SENT ME TO JERUSALEM

NEHEMIAH 2:1-10, PSALM 137, HEBREWS 12:18-24

NEHEMIAH 2:1–10

Nehemiah Sent to Jerusalem

1 During the month of Nisan in the twentieth year of King Artaxerxes,
when wine was set before him, I took the wine and gave it to the king.
I had never been sad in his presence, 2 so the king said to me, "Why are
you sad, when you aren't sick? This is nothing but sadness of heart."

I was overwhelmed with fear 3 and replied to the king, "May the king live
forever! Why should I not be sad when the city where my ancestors are
buried lies in ruins and its gates have been destroyed by fire?"

4 Then the king asked me, "What is your request?"

So I prayed to the God of the heavens 5 and answered the king, "If it
pleases the king, and if your servant has found favor with you, send me
to Judah and to the city where my ancestors are buried, so that I may
rebuild it."

6 The king, with the queen seated beside him, asked me, "How long will
your journey take, and when will you return?" So I gave him a definite
time, and it pleased the king to send me.

7 I also said to the king: "If it pleases the king, let me have letters written
to the governors of the region west of the Euphrates River, so that they
will grant me safe passage until I reach Judah. 8 And let me have a letter
written to Asaph, keeper of the king's forest, so that he will give me
timber to rebuild the gates of the temple's fortress, the city wall, and the
home where I will live." The king granted my requests, for the gracious
hand of my God was on me.

9 I went to the governors of the region west of the Euphrates and gave
them the king's letters. The king had also sent officers of the infantry
and cavalry with me. 10 When Sanballat the Horonite and Tobiah the
Ammonite official heard that someone had come to pursue the prosperity
of the Israelites, they were greatly displeased.

NOTES

PSALM 137

Lament of the Exiles

1 BY THE RIVERS OF BABYLON—
THERE WE SAT DOWN AND WEPT
WHEN WE REMEMBERED ZION.

2 There we hung up our lyres
on the poplar trees,
3 for our captors there asked us for songs,
and our tormentors, for rejoicing:
"Sing us one of the songs of Zion."

4 How can we sing the LORD's song
on foreign soil?
5 If I forget you, Jerusalem,
may my right hand forget its skill.
6 May my tongue stick to the roof of my mouth
if I do not remember you,
if I do not exalt Jerusalem as my greatest joy!

7 Remember, LORD, what the Edomites said
that day at Jerusalem:
"Destroy it! Destroy it
down to its foundations!"
8 Daughter Babylon, doomed to destruction,
happy is the one who pays you back
what you have done to us.
9 Happy is he who takes your little ones
and dashes them against the rocks.

HEBREWS 12:18–24

18 For you have not come to what could be touched, to a blazing fire, to
darkness, gloom, and storm, 19 to the blast of a trumpet, and the sound
of words. Those who heard it begged that not another word be spoken
to them, 20 for they could not bear what was commanded: If even an
animal touches the mountain, it must be stoned. 21 The appearance was

TITLE

THE WALLS OF JERUSALEM

ITEM 1

NEHEMIAH'S JERUSALEM

DOCUMENT TYPE

MAP

DATE

444 BC

Nehemiah's Jerusalem was small–not much larger than than the footprint of a shopping mall and its surrounding parking lot. When Nehemiah set out to rebuild the city walls, he was not just repairing what had been destroyed: he was reconstructing the place where many of the events of the New Testament would one day occur. Though the walls were later expanded, Nehemiah's faith and his work to rebuild the city walls played a crucial role in the survival of Jerusalem as Israel's capital city.

Keep the map on the back of this page open to guide you as you read.

FLIP TO VIEW →

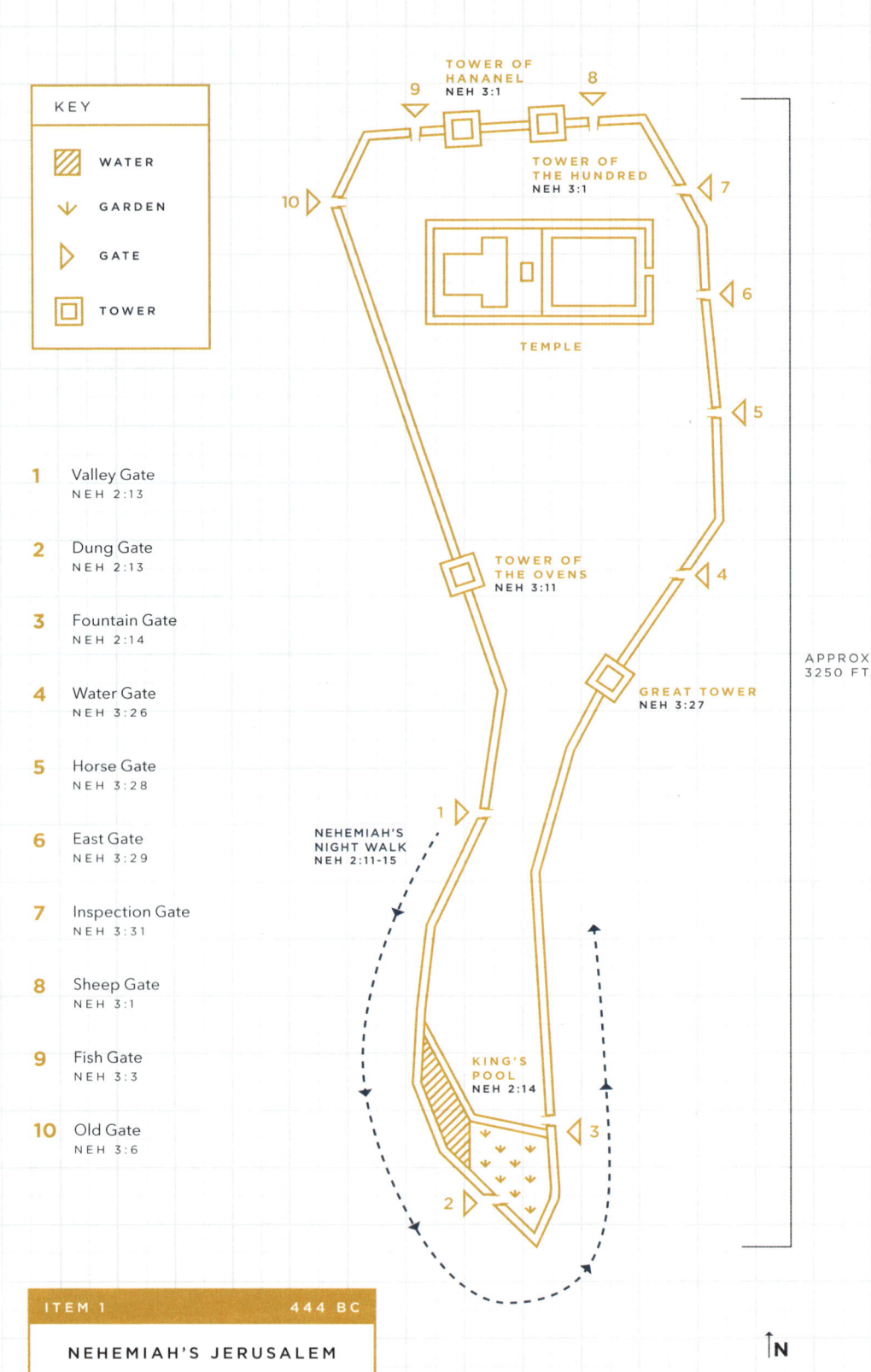

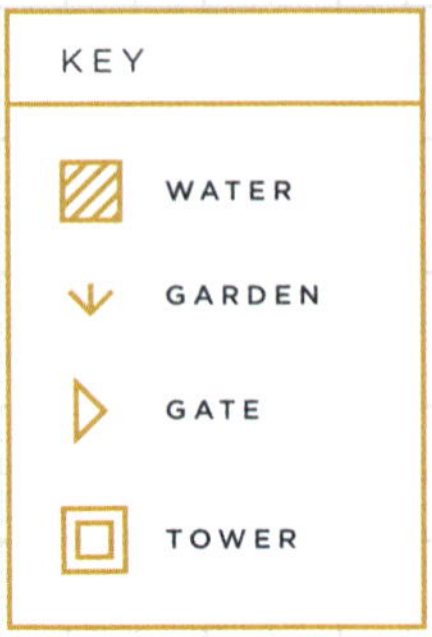
KEY
WATER
GARDEN
GATE
TOWER

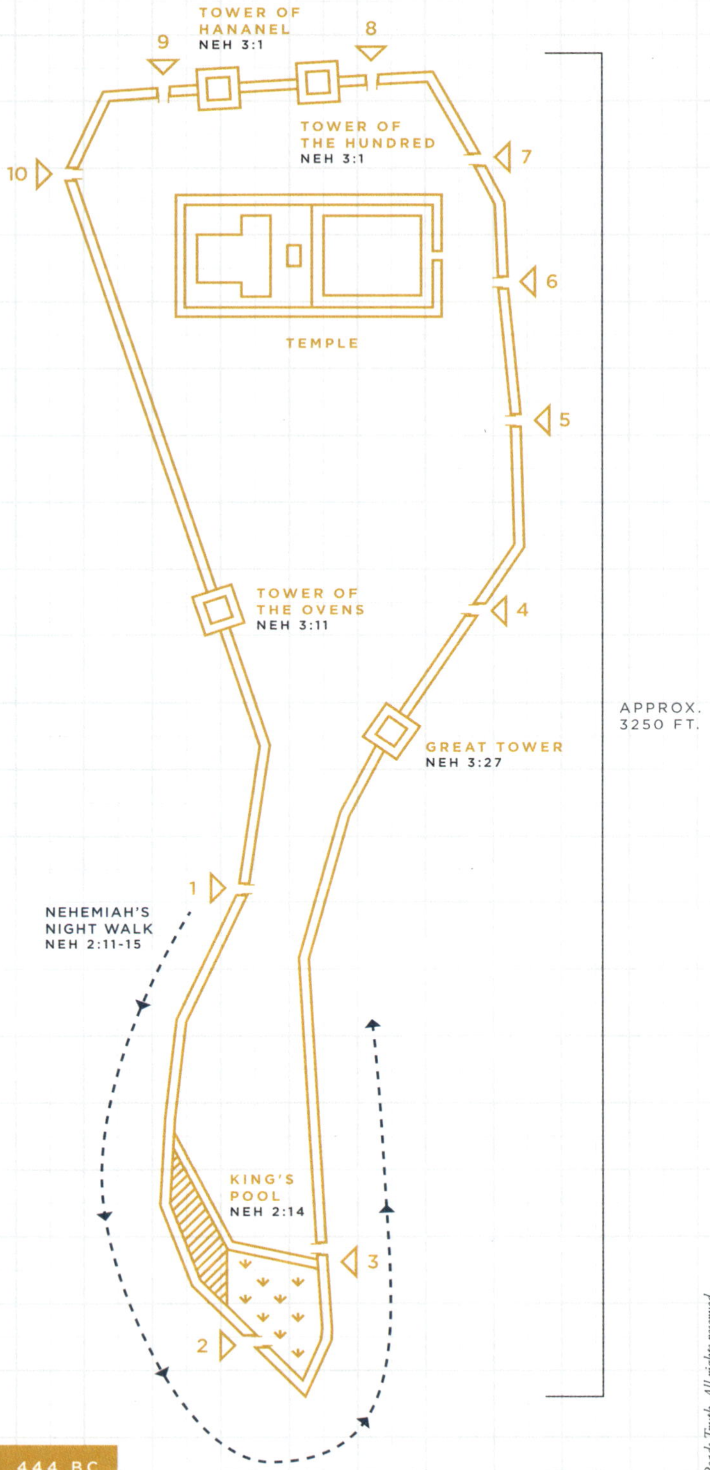
TOWER OF HANANEL
NEH 3:1
9
8
TOWER OF THE HUNDRED
NEH 3:1
7
10
TEMPLE
6
5
TOWER OF THE OVENS
NEH 3:11
4
APPROX. 3250 FT.
GREAT TOWER
NEH 3:27
1
NEHEMIAH'S NIGHT WALK
NEH 2:11-15
KING'S POOL
NEH 2:14
3
2

1 Valley Gate
NEH 2:13

2 Dung Gate
NEH 2:13

3 Fountain Gate
NEH 2:14

4 Water Gate
NEH 3:26

5 Horse Gate
NEH 3:28

6 East Gate
NEH 3:29

7 Inspection Gate
NEH 3:31

8 Sheep Gate
NEH 3:1

9 Fish Gate
NEH 3:3

10 Old Gate
NEH 3:6

ITEM 1 444 BC

NEHEMIAH'S JERUSALEM

N

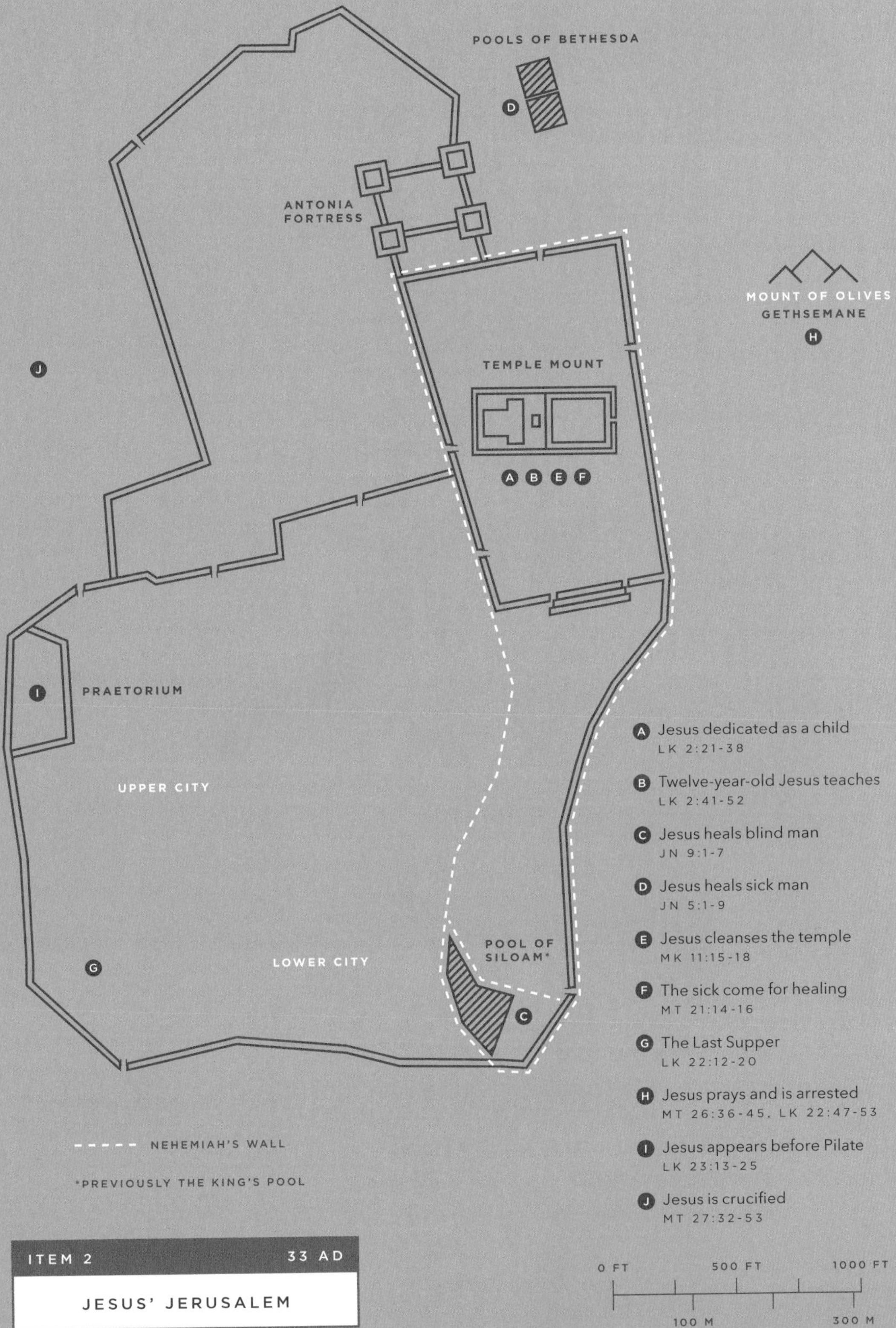
POOLS OF BETHESDA
D
ANTONIA FORTRESS
MOUNT OF OLIVES
GETHSEMANE
H
J
TEMPLE MOUNT
A B E F
PRAETORIUM
I
UPPER CITY
LOWER CITY
POOL OF SILOAM*
C
G
A Jesus dedicated as a child
LK 2:21-38
B Twelve-year-old Jesus teaches
LK 2:41-52
C Jesus heals blind man
JN 9:1-7
D Jesus heals sick man
JN 5:1-9
E Jesus cleanses the temple
MK 11:15-18
F The sick come for healing
MT 21:14-16
G The Last Supper
LK 22:12-20
H Jesus prays and is arrested
MT 26:36-45, LK 22:47-53
I Jesus appears before Pilate
LK 23:13-25
J Jesus is crucified
MT 27:32-53
NEHEMIAH'S WALL
*PREVIOUSLY THE KING'S POOL
0 FT
500 FT
1000 FT
100 M
300 M

ITEM 2 33 AD

JESUS' JERUSALEM

so terrifying that Moses said, I am trembling with fear. [22] Instead, you have come to Mount Zion, to the city of the living God (the heavenly Jerusalem), to myriads of angels, a festive gathering, [23] to the assembly of the firstborn whose names have been written in heaven, to a Judge, who is God of all, to the spirits of righteous people made perfect, [24] and to Jesus, the mediator of a new covenant, and to the sprinkled blood, which says better things than the blood of Abel.

ITEM 2

JESUS' JERUSALEM

DOCUMENT TYPE

MAP

DATE

AD 33

The centerpiece of the Christian faith—the death and resurrection of Jesus—took place in Jerusalem just a few hundred years after the time of Nehemiah. Jerusalem saw many changes between the time of Nehemiah and the time of Christ. The city grew and new walls were built. The Romans brought technological advances like aqueducts and improved methods of paving. But the site itself remained a key location in the unfolding story of our redemption.

This map shows Nehemiah's walls overlayed onto the Jerusalem where Jesus ministered, died, and rose again.

CRAFTSMAN
NICKEL PLATED

3

WE PREPARED TO REBUILD THE WALLS

NEHEMIAH 2:11-20, ISAIAH 62:8-12, EPHESIANS 2:19-22, JAMES 2:14-26

NEHEMIAH 2:11–20

Preparing to Rebuild the Walls

11 After I arrived in Jerusalem and had been there three days, 12 I got up at
night and took a few men with me. I didn't tell anyone what my God had
laid on my heart to do for Jerusalem. The only animal I took was the one
I was riding. 13 I went out at night through the Valley Gate toward the
Serpent's Well and the Dung Gate, and I inspected the walls of Jerusalem
that had been broken down and its gates that had been destroyed by fire.
14 I went on to the Fountain Gate and the King's Pool, but farther down
it became too narrow for my animal to go through. 15 So I went up at
night by way of the valley and inspected the wall. Then heading back,
I entered through the Valley Gate and returned. 16 The officials did not
know where I had gone or what I was doing, for I had not yet told the
Jews, priests, nobles, officials, or the rest of those who would be doing the
work. 17 So I said to them, "You see the trouble we are in. Jerusalem lies in
ruins and its gates have been burned. Come, let's rebuild Jerusalem's wall,
so that we will no longer be a disgrace." 18 I told them how the gracious
hand of my God had been on me, and what the king had said to me.

THEY SAID, "LET'S START REBUILDING," AND THEIR HANDS WERE STRENGTHENED TO DO THIS GOOD WORK.

19 When Sanballat the Horonite, Tobiah the Ammonite official, and
Geshem the Arab heard about this, they mocked and despised us, and
said, "What is this you're doing? Are you rebelling against the king?"

20 I gave them this reply, "The God of the heavens is the one who will
grant us success. We, his servants, will start building, but you have no
share, right, or historic claim in Jerusalem."

ISAIAH 62:8–12

8 The LORD has sworn with his right hand
and his strong arm:
I will no longer give your grain
to your enemies for food,
and foreigners will not drink the new wine
for which you have labored.

NOTES

[9] For those who gather grain will eat it
and praise the Lord,
and those who harvest the grapes will drink the wine
in my holy courts.

[10] Go out, go out through the city gates;
prepare a way for the people!
Build it up, build up the highway;
clear away the stones!
Raise a banner for the peoples.
[11] Look, the Lord has proclaimed
to the ends of the earth,
"Say to Daughter Zion:
Look, your salvation is coming,
his wages are with him,
and his reward accompanies him."
[12] And they will be called the Holy People,
the Lord's Redeemed;
and you will be called Cared For,
A City Not Deserted.

EPHESIANS 2:19–22

[19] So then you are no longer foreigners and strangers, but fellow citizens
with the saints, and members of God's household, [20] built on the
foundation of the apostles and prophets, with Christ Jesus himself as the
cornerstone. [21] In him the whole building, being put together, grows into
a holy temple in the Lord. [22] In him you are also being built together for
God's dwelling in the Spirit.

JAMES 2:14–26

Faith and Works

[14] What good is it, my brothers and sisters, if someone claims to have faith but does not have works? Can such faith save him?

NOTES

[15] If a brother or sister is without clothes and lacks daily food [16] and one
of you says to them, "Go in peace, stay warm, and be well fed," but you
don't give them what the body needs, what good is it? [17] In the same way
faith, if it doesn't have works, is dead by itself.

[18] But someone will say, "You have faith, and I have works." Show
me your faith without works, and I will show you faith by my works.
[19] You believe that God is one. Good! Even the demons believe—and
they shudder.

[20] Senseless person! Are you willing to learn that faith without works
is useless? [21] Wasn't Abraham our father justified by works in offering
Isaac his son on the altar? [22] You see that faith was active together with
his works, and by works, faith was made complete, [23] and the Scripture
was fulfilled that says, Abraham believed God, and it was credited to him
as righteousness, and he was called God's friend. [24] You see that a person
is justified by works and not by faith alone. [25] In the same way, wasn't
Rahab the prostitute also justified by works in receiving the messengers
and sending them out by a different route? [26] For just as the body without
the spirit is dead, so also faith without works is dead.

4 WE BEGAN REBUILDING THE WALLS

NEHEMIAH 3, ROMANS 12:3–8, PSALM 8:1

NEHEMIAH 3

Rebuilding the Walls

1 The high priest Eliashib and his fellow priests began rebuilding the Sheep Gate.
They dedicated it and installed its doors. After building the wall to the Tower of the
Hundred and the Tower of Hananel, they dedicated it. 2 The men of Jericho built
next to Eliashib, and next to them Zaccur son of Imri built.

Fish Gate

3 The sons of Hassenaah built the Fish Gate. They built it with beams and installed
its doors, bolts, and bars. 4 Next to them Meremoth son of Uriah, son of Hakkoz,
made repairs. Beside them Meshullam son of Berechiah, son of Meshezabel, made
repairs. Next to them Zadok son of Baana made repairs. 5 Beside them the Tekoites
made repairs, but their nobles did not lift a finger to help their supervisors.

Old Gate, Broad Wall, and Tower of the Ovens

6 Joiada son of Paseah and Meshullam son of Besodeiah repaired the Old Gate.
They built it with beams and installed its doors, bolts, and bars. 7 Next to them the
repairs were done by Melatiah the Gibeonite, Jadon the Meronothite, and the men
of Gibeon and Mizpah, who were under the authority of the governor of the region
west of the Euphrates River. 8 After him Uzziel son of Harhaiah, the goldsmith,
made repairs, and next to him Hananiah son of the perfumer made repairs. They
restored Jerusalem as far as the Broad Wall.

[9] Next to them Rephaiah son of Hur, ruler of half the district of Jerusalem, made repairs. [10] After them Jedaiah son of Harumaph made repairs across from his house. Next to him Hattush the son of Hashabneiah made repairs. [11] Malchijah son of Harim and Hasshub son of Pahath-moab made repairs to another section, as well as to the Tower of the Ovens.

NOTES

[12] BESIDE HIM SHALLUM SON OF HALLOHESH, RULER OF HALF THE DISTRICT OF JERUSALEM, MADE REPAIRS—HE AND HIS DAUGHTERS.

Valley Gate, Dung Gate, and Fountain Gate

[13] Hanun and the inhabitants of Zanoah repaired the Valley Gate. They rebuilt it and installed its doors, bolts, and bars, and repaired five hundred yards of the wall to the Dung Gate. [14] Malchijah son of Rechab, ruler of the district of Beth-haccherem, repaired the Dung Gate. He rebuilt it and installed its doors, bolts, and bars.

[15] Shallun son of Col-hozeh, ruler of the district of Mizpah, repaired the Fountain Gate. He rebuilt it and roofed it. Then he installed its doors, bolts, and bars. He also made repairs to the wall of the Pool of Shelah near the king's garden, as far as the stairs that descend from the city of David.

[16] After him Nehemiah son of Azbuk, ruler of half the district of Beth-zur, made repairs up to a point opposite the tombs of David, as far as the artificial pool and the House of the Warriors. [17] Next to him the Levites made repairs under Rehum son of Bani. Beside him Hashabiah, ruler of half the district of Keilah, made repairs for his district. [18] After him their fellow Levites made repairs under Binnui son of Henadad, ruler of half the district of Keilah. [19] Next to him Ezer son of Jeshua, ruler of Mizpah, made repairs to another section opposite the ascent to the armory at the Angle.

The Angle, Water Gate, and Tower on the Ophel

[20] After him Baruch son of Zabbai diligently repaired another section, from the Angle to the door of the house of the high priest Eliashib. [21] Beside him Meremoth son of Uriah, son of Hakkoz, made repairs to another section, from the door of Eliashib's house to the end of his house.

425,- Pr. kg.

[22] And next to him the priests from the surrounding area made repairs.

[23] After them Benjamin and Hasshub made repairs opposite their house.
Beside them Azariah son of Maaseiah, son of Ananiah, made repairs
beside his house. [24] After him Binnui son of Henadad made repairs to
another section, from the house of Azariah to the Angle and the corner.
[25] Palal son of Uzai made repairs opposite the Angle and tower that juts
out from the king's upper palace, by the courtyard of the guard. Beside
him Pedaiah son of Parosh [26] and the temple servants living on Ophel
made repairs opposite the Water Gate toward the east and the tower that
juts out. [27] Next to him the Tekoites made repairs to another section from
a point opposite the great tower that juts out, as far as the wall of Ophel.

NOTES

Horse Gate, Inspection Gate, and Sheep Gate

[28] Each of the priests made repairs above the Horse Gate, each opposite
his own house. [29] After them Zadok son of Immer made repairs opposite
his house. And beside him Shemaiah son of Shecaniah, guard of the
East Gate, made repairs. [30] Next to him Hananiah son of Shelemiah and
Hanun the sixth son of Zalaph made repairs to another section.

After them Meshullam son of Berechiah made repairs opposite his room.
[31] Next to him Malchijah, one of the goldsmiths, made repairs to the
house of the temple servants and the merchants, opposite the Inspection
Gate, and as far as the upstairs room on the corner. [32] The goldsmiths
and merchants made repairs between the upstairs room on the corner
and the Sheep Gate.

ROMANS 12:3–8

Many Gifts but One Body

[3] For by the grace given to me, I tell everyone among you not to think of himself more highly than he should think. Instead, think sensibly, as God has distributed a measure of faith to each one.

[4] NOW AS WE HAVE MANY PARTS IN ONE
BODY, AND ALL THE PARTS DO NOT HAVE
THE SAME FUNCTION, [5] IN THE SAME WAY
WE WHO ARE MANY ARE ONE BODY IN
CHRIST AND INDIVIDUALLY MEMBERS OF
ONE ANOTHER.

[6] According to the grace given to us, we have different gifts: If prophecy,
use it according to the proportion of one's faith; [7] if service, use it in
service; if teaching, in teaching; [8] if exhorting, in exhortation; giving, with
generosity; leading, with diligence; showing mercy, with cheerfulness.

PSALM 8:1

Lord, our Lord,
how magnificent is your name throughout the earth!
You have covered the heavens with your majesty.

NEHEMIAH 4

Progress in Spite of Opposition

1 When Sanballat heard that we were rebuilding the wall, he became
furious. He mocked the Jews 2 before his colleagues and the powerful
men of Samaria, and said, "What are these pathetic Jews doing? Can they
restore it by themselves? Will they offer sacrifices? Will they ever finish it?

CAN THEY BRING THESE BURNT STONES BACK TO LIFE FROM THE MOUNDS OF RUBBLE?"

3 Then Tobiah the Ammonite, who was beside him, said, "Indeed, even if a fox climbed up what they are building, he would break down their stone wall!"

4 Listen, our God, for we are despised. Make their insults return on their
own heads and let them be taken as plunder to a land of captivity. 5 Do not
cover their guilt or let their sin be erased from your sight, because they have angered the builders.

6 So we rebuilt the wall until the entire wall was joined together up to half its height, for the people had the will to keep working.

7 When Sanballat, Tobiah, and the Arabs, Ammonites, and Ashdodites
heard that the repair to the walls of Jerusalem was progressing and that the
gaps were being closed, they became furious. 8 They all plotted together
to come and fight against Jerusalem and throw it into confusion. 9 So we
prayed to our God and stationed a guard because of them day and night.

10 In Judah, it was said:

The strength of the laborer fails,
since there is so much rubble.
We will never be able
to rebuild the wall.

11 And our enemies said, "They won't realize it until we're among them
and can kill them and stop the work." 12 When the Jews who lived nearby
arrived, they said to us time and again, "Everywhere you turn, they

NOTES

attack us." [13] So I stationed people behind the lowest sections of the wall,
at the vulnerable areas. I stationed them by families with their swords,
spears, and bows. [14] After I made an inspection, I stood up and said to
the nobles, the officials, and the rest of the people, "Don't be afraid of
them. Remember the great and awe-inspiring Lord, and fight for your
countrymen, your sons and daughters, your wives and homes."

Sword and Trowel

[15] When our enemies heard that we knew their scheme and that God
had frustrated it, every one of us returned to his own work on the wall.

[16] FROM THAT DAY ON, HALF OF MY MEN DID THE WORK WHILE THE OTHER HALF HELD SPEARS, SHIELDS, BOWS, AND ARMOR.

The officers supported all the people of Judah, [17] who were rebuilding the
wall. The laborers who carried the loads worked with one hand and held
a weapon with the other. [18] Each of the builders had his sword strapped
around his waist while he was building, and the trumpeter was beside
me. [19] Then I said to the nobles, the officials, and the rest of the people:
"The work is enormous and spread out, and we are separated far from
one another along the wall. [20] Wherever you hear the trumpet sound,
rally to us there. Our God will fight for us!" [21] So we continued the work,
while half of the men were holding spears from daybreak until the stars
came out. [22] At that time, I also said to the people, "Let everyone and his
servant spend the night inside Jerusalem, so that they can stand guard by
night and work by day." [23] And I, my brothers, my servants, and the men
of the guard with me never took off our clothes. Each carried his weapon,
even when washing.

GENESIS 28:15

"Look, I am with you and will watch over you wherever you go. I will bring you back to this land, for I will not leave you until I have done what I have promised you."

[18] I pray that the eyes of your heart may be enlightened so that you may
know what is the hope of his calling, what is the wealth of his glorious
inheritance in the saints, [19] and what is the immeasurable greatness of
his power toward us who believe, according to the mighty working of
his strength.

God's Power in Christ

[20] He exercised this power in Christ by raising him from the dead and
seating him at his right hand in the heavens— [21] far above every ruler and
authority, power and dominion, and every title given, not only in this age
but also in the one to come. [22] And he subjected everything under his feet
and appointed him as head over everything for the church, [23] which is his
body, the fullness of the one who fills all things in every way.

TITLE

NEHEMIAH AND THE BABYLONIAN CAPTIVITY

DOCUMENT TYPE

TIMELINE

Why was Nehemiah in the city of Susa in the first place? Why was he serving as the cupbearer to King Artaxerxes? This timeline details how the people of Judah came to be living as exiles under the rule of a Persian king, starting with the division of Israel in 931 BC and ending with Nehemiah's return to Jerusalem almost 500 years later.

931 BC

Israel becomes a divided kingdom under King Solomon's son, Rehoboam. The northern tribes become the northern kingdom, and the tribes of Judah and Benjamin become the southern kingdom.

1 KINGS 12
2 CHRONICLES 10

722 BC

The northern kingdom is taken into captivity by the Assyrians, leaving only the southern kingdom.

2 KINGS 17–18

605 BC

Young men from prominent families in Judah are taken into captivity in Babylon. This includes Daniel, Hananiah, Mishael, and Azariah, who are assigned the names Belteshazzar, Shadrach, Meshach, and Abednego by the Babylonians.

DANIEL 1:1–7

700

60

c. 597 BC

Babylon, led by King Nebuchadnezzar, begins a three-month siege of Judah's capital city, Jerusalem. The Babylonians pillage Jerusalem and claim the southern kingdom.

PSALM 137

c. 587 BC

Judah's king, Zedekiah, revolts against Babylonian control. King Nebuchadnezzar responds by destroying Jerusalem, along with its temple and city walls.

2 KINGS 24:10-25:21

c. 586 BC

The rest of the tribe of Judah is carried off into captivity by the Babylonians. The exiles from Judah become servants of the Babylonians, and many marry Babylonians.

2 CHRONICLES 36:20
JEREMIAH 29; 52

539 BC

Under the rule of King Cyrus, the kingdom of Persia conquers Babylon, inheriting the exiles of Judah.

2 CHRONICLES 36:20-21

538 BC

Compelled by the Holy Spirit, King Cyrus issues a decree stating that anyone from Judah can return home without penalty, the temple in Jerusalem is to be rebuilt, Cyrus's royal treasury will fund the work, and anything King Nebuchadnezzar took from the temple is to be returned.

EZRA 1-6

c. 515 BC

King Darius issues a decree that allows the Jewish people to finish building the temple without interruption. The temple, commonly referred to as the "second temple," is completed in Jerusalem under the leadership of Zerubbabel and the prophets Haggai and Zechariah.

EZRA 6:16-23

c. 479 BC

Esther becomes queen of Persia after marrying King Ahasuerus. As queen, Esther uses her influence to stop the Persians from persecuting the Jewish people.

ESTHER 2:16-18

458 BC

A new Persian king, Artaxerxes I, issues a decree declaring that the exiles living in Persia are free to return home to Judah. Nehemiah remains in Persia, eventually becoming the royal cupbearer for King Artaxerxes.

EZRA 7-10

444 BC

While serving in the Persian city of Susa, Nehemiah learns that Jerusalem is still in great disrepair. When he hears the news, he asks the Lord to give him favor with King Artaxerxes so he can return to Jerusalem to repair its walls and gates.

NEHEMIAH 1-13

500

6

GRACE DAY

Use today to pray, rest, and reflect on this week's reading, giving thanks for the grace that is ours in Christ.

LORD, OUR LORD, HOW MAGNIFICENT IS YOUR NAME THROUGHOUT THE EARTH! YOU HAVE COVERED THE HEAVENS WITH YOUR MAJESTY.

PSALM 8:1

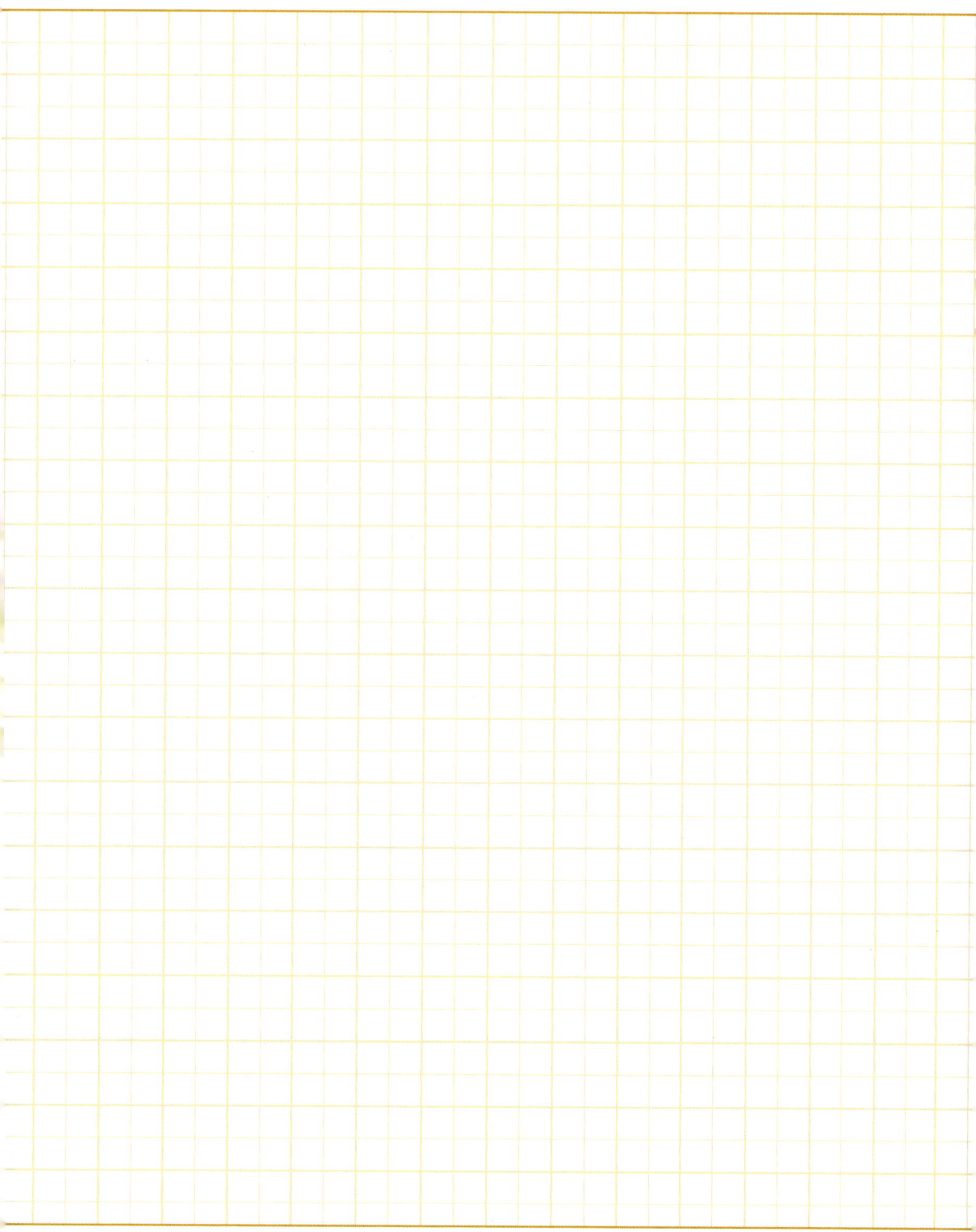

7

WEEKLY TRUTH

Scripture is God-breathed and true. When we memorize it, we carry the gospel with us wherever we go.

This week we will memorize the key verse for the book of Nehemiah.

SO I SAID TO THEM, "YOU SEE THE TROUBLE WE ARE IN. JERUSALEM LIES IN RUINS AND ITS GATES HAVE BEEN BURNED. COME, LET'S REBUILD JERUSALEM'S WALL, SO THAT WE WILL NO LONGER BE A DISGRACE."

NEHEMIAH 2:17

Find the corresponding memory card in the back of your book.

8

I STOOD AGAINST SOCIAL INJUSTICE

NEHEMIAH 5, EXODUS 22:25, 2 CORINTHIANS 8:9

NEHEMIAH 5

Social Injustice

1 There was a widespread outcry from the people and their wives against
their Jewish countrymen. 2 Some were saying, "We, our sons, and our
daughters are numerous. Let us get grain so that we can eat and live."
3 Others were saying, "We are mortgaging our fields, vineyards, and
homes to get grain during the famine." 4 Still others were saying, "We
have borrowed money to pay the king's tax on our fields and vineyards.
5 We and our children are just like our countrymen and their children,
yet we are subjecting our sons and daughters to slavery. Some of our
daughters are already enslaved, but we are powerless because our fields
and vineyards belong to others."

6 I became extremely angry when I heard their outcry and these
complaints. 7 After seriously considering the matter, I accused the nobles
and officials, saying to them, "Each of you is charging his countrymen
interest." So I called a large assembly against them 8 and said, "We have
done our best to buy back our Jewish countrymen who were sold to
foreigners, but now you sell your own countrymen, and we have to buy
them back." They remained silent and could not say a word. 9 Then
I said, "What you are doing isn't right.

SHOULDN'T YOU WALK IN THE FEAR OF OUR GOD AND NOT INVITE THE REPROACH OF OUR FOREIGN ENEMIES?

10 Even I, as well as my brothers and my servants, have been lending them
money and grain. Please, let us stop charging this interest. 11 Return their
fields, vineyards, olive groves, and houses to them immediately, along
with the percentage of the money, grain, new wine, and fresh oil that you
have been assessing them."

12 They responded: "We will return these things and require nothing
more from them. We will do as you say."

So I summoned the priests and made everyone take an oath to do this.
13 I also shook the folds of my robe and said, "May God likewise shake
from his house and property everyone who doesn't keep this promise.
May he be shaken out and have nothing!"

The whole assembly said, "Amen," and they praised the LORD. Then the people did as they had promised.

NOTES

Good and Bad Governors

[14] Furthermore, from the day King Artaxerxes appointed me to be their governor in the land of Judah—from the twentieth year until his thirty-second year, twelve years—I and my associates never ate from the food allotted to the governor. [15] The governors who preceded me had heavily burdened the people, taking from them food and wine as well as a pound of silver. Their subordinates also oppressed the people, but because of the fear of God, I didn't do this. [16] Instead, I devoted myself to the construction of this wall, and all my subordinates were gathered there for the work. We didn't buy any land.

[17] There were 150 Jews and officials, as well as guests from the surrounding nations at my table. [18] Each day, one ox, six choice sheep, and some fowl were prepared for me. An abundance of all kinds of wine was provided every ten days. But I didn't demand the food allotted to the governor, because the burden on the people was so heavy.

[19] Remember me favorably, my God, for all that I have done for this people.

EXODUS 22:25

"If you lend silver to my people, to the poor person among you, you must not be like a creditor to him; you must not charge him interest."

2 CORINTHIANS 8:9

For you know the grace of our Lord Jesus Christ: Though he was rich, for your sake he became poor, so that by his poverty you might become rich.

9

WE COMPLETED THE WALL

NEHEMIAH 6, ISAIAH 9:6-7, JEREMIAH 23:5-6

NEHEMIAH 6

Attempts to Discourage the Builders

1 When Sanballat, Tobiah, Geshem the Arab, and the rest of our enemies
heard that I had rebuilt the wall and that no gap was left in it—though at
that time I had not installed the doors in the city gates— 2 Sanballat and
Geshem sent me a message: "Come, let's meet together in the villages of
the Ono Valley." They were planning to harm me.

3 So I sent messengers to them, saying,

"I AM DOING IMPORTANT WORK AND CANNOT COME DOWN.

Why should the work cease while I leave it and go down to you?" 4 Four
times they sent me the same proposal, and I gave them the same reply.

5 Sanballat sent me this same message a fifth time by his aide, who had an
open letter in his hand. 6 In it was written:

> It is reported among the nations—and Geshem agrees—that you and
> the Jews plan to rebel. This is the reason you are building the wall.
> According to these reports, you are to become their king 7 and have
> even set up the prophets in Jerusalem to proclaim on your behalf:
> "There is a king in Judah." These rumors will be heard by the king.
> So come, let's confer together.

8 Then I replied to him, "There is nothing to these rumors you are
spreading; you are inventing them in your own mind." 9 For they were
all trying to intimidate us, saying, "They will drop their hands from the
work, and it will never be finished."

But now, my God, strengthen my hands.

Attempts to Intimidate Nehemiah

10 I went to the house of Shemaiah son of Delaiah, son of Mehetabel,
who was restricted to his house. He said:

NOTES

Let's meet at the house of God,
inside the temple.
Let's shut the temple doors
because they're coming to kill you.
They're coming to kill you tonight!

11 But I said, "Should a man like me run away? How can someone like me enter the temple and live? I will not go."
12 I realized that God had not sent him, because of the prophecy he spoke against me. Tobiah and Sanballat had hired him.
13 He was hired, so that I would be intimidated, do as he suggested, sin, and get a bad reputation, in order that they could discredit me.

14 My God, remember Tobiah and Sanballat for what they have done, and also the prophetess Noadiah and the other prophets who wanted to intimidate me.

The Wall Completed

15 The wall was completed in fifty-two days, on the twenty-fifth day of the month Elul.
16 When all our enemies heard this, all the surrounding nations were intimidated and lost their confidence,

FOR THEY REALIZED THAT THIS TASK HAD BEEN ACCOMPLISHED BY OUR GOD.

17 During those days, the nobles of Judah sent many letters to Tobiah, and Tobiah's letters came to them.
18 For many in Judah were bound by oath to him, since he was a son-in-law of Shecaniah son of Arah, and his son Jehohanan had married the daughter of Meshullam son of Berechiah.
19 These nobles kept mentioning Tobiah's good deeds to me, and they reported my words to him. And Tobiah sent letters to intimidate me.

ISAIAH 9:6–7

6 For a child will be born for us,
a son will be given to us,
and the government will be on his shoulders.
He will be named

NOTES

Wonderful Counselor, Mighty God,
Eternal Father, Prince of Peace.
7 The dominion will be vast,
and its prosperity will never end.
He will reign on the throne of David
and over his kingdom,
to establish and sustain it
with justice and righteousness from now on and forever.
The zeal of the LORD of Armies will accomplish this.

JEREMIAH 23:5–6

The Righteous Branch of David
5 "Look, the days are coming"—this is the LORD declaration—
"when I will raise up a Righteous Branch for David.
He will reign wisely as king
and administer justice and righteousness in the land.

6 IN HIS DAYS JUDAH WILL BE SAVED,
AND ISRAEL WILL DWELL SECURELY.

This is the name he will be called:
The LORD Is Our Righteousness."

10

THE EXILES CAME BACK HOME

NEHEMIAH 7:1-73a, EXODUS 28:29-30, PSALM 34:19-22

NEHEMIAH 7:1–73a

The Exiles Return

1 When the wall had been rebuilt and I had the doors installed, the
gatekeepers, singers, and Levites were appointed. 2 Then I put my brother
Hanani in charge of Jerusalem, along with Hananiah, commander of the
fortress, because he was a faithful man who feared God more than most.
3 I said to them, "Do not open the gates of Jerusalem until the sun is hot,
and let the doors be shut and securely fastened while the guards are on
duty. Station the citizens of Jerusalem as guards, some at their posts and
some at their homes."

4 The city was large and spacious, but there were few people in it, and
no houses had been built yet. 5 Then my God put it into my mind to
assemble the nobles, the officials, and the people to be registered by
genealogy. I found the genealogical record of those who came back first,
and I found the following written in it:

6 These are the people of the province who went up among the captive
exiles deported by King Nebuchadnezzar of Babylon. Each of them
returned to Jerusalem and Judah, to his own town. 7 They came with
Zerubbabel, Jeshua, Nehemiah, Azariah, Raamiah, Nahamani, Mordecai,
Bilshan, Mispereth, Bigvai, Nehum, and Baanah.

The number of the Israelite men included

8 Parosh's descendants	2,172
9 Shephatiah's descendants	372
10 Arah's descendants	652
11 Pahath-moab's descendants:	
Jeshua's and Joab's descendants	2,818
12 Elam's descendants	1,254
13 Zattu's descendants	845
14 Zaccai's descendants	760
15 Binnui's descendants	648
16 Bebai's descendants	628
17 Azgad's descendants	2,322

18 Adonikam's descendants	667
19 Bigvai's descendants	2,067
20 Adin's descendants	655
21 Ater's descendants: of Hezekiah	98
22 Hashum's descendants	328
23 Bezai's descendants	324
24 Hariph's descendants	112
25 Gibeon's descendants	95
26 Bethlehem's and Netophah's men	188
27 Anathoth's men	128
28 Beth-azmaveth's men	42
29 Kiriath-jearim's, Chephirah's, and Beeroth's men	743
30 Ramah's and Geba's men	621
31 Michmas's men	122
32 Bethel's and Ai's men	123
33 the other Nebo's men	52
34 the other Elam's people	1,254
35 Harim's people	320
36 Jericho's people	345
37 Lod's, Hadid's, and Ono's people	721
38 Senaah's people	3,930.

39 The priests included

Jedaiah's descendants of the house of Jeshua	973
40 Immer's descendants	1,052
41 Pashhur's descendants	1,247
42 Harim's descendants	1,017.

43 The Levites included

Jeshua's descendants: of Kadmiel	
Hodevah's descendants	74.

44 The singers included

Asaph's descendants	148.

45 The gatekeepers included
Shallum's descendants, Ater's descendants,
Talmon's descendants, Akkub's descendants,
Hatita's descendants, Shobai's descendants 138.

46 The temple servants included
Ziha's descendants, Hasupha's descendants,
Tabbaoth's descendants, 47 Keros's descendants,
Sia's descendants, Padon's descendants,
48 Lebanah's descendants, Hagabah's descendants,
Shalmai's descendants, 49 Hanan's descendants,
Giddel's descendants, Gahar's descendants,
50 Reaiah's descendants, Rezin's descendants,
Nekoda's descendants, 51 Gazzam's descendants,
Uzza's descendants, Paseah's descendants,
52 Besai's descendants, Meunim's descendants,
Nephishesim's descendants, 53 Bakbuk's descendants,
Hakupha's descendants, Harhur's descendants,
54 Bazlith's descendants, Mehida's descendants,
Harsha's descendants, 55 Barkos's descendants,
Sisera's descendants, Temah's descendants,
56 Neziah's descendants, Hatipha's descendants.

57 The descendants of Solomon's servants included
Sotai's descendants, Sophereth's descendants,
Perida's descendants, 58 Jaala's descendants,
Darkon's descendants, Giddel's descendants,
59 Shephatiah's descendants, Hattil's descendants,
Pochereth-hazzebaim's descendants, Amon's descendants.

60 All the temple servants
and the descendants of Solomon's servants 392.

NOTES

[61] The following are those who came from Tel-melah, Tel-harsha, Cherub, Addon, and Immer, but were unable to prove that their ancestral families and their lineage were Israelite:

[62] Delaiah's descendants,
Tobiah's descendants,
and Nekoda's descendants 642

[63] and from the priests: the descendants of Hobaiah, the descendants of Hakkoz, and the descendants of Barzillai—who had taken a wife from the daughters of Barzillai the Gileadite and who bore their name. [64] These searched for their entries in the genealogical records, but they could not be found, so they were disqualified from the priesthood. [65] The governor ordered them not to eat the most holy things until there was a priest who could consult the Urim and Thummim.

[66] The whole combined assembly numbered 42,360 [67] not including their 7,337 male and female servants, as well as their 245 male and female singers. [68] They had 736 horses, 245 mules, [69] 435 camels, and 6,720 donkeys.

[70] Some of the family heads contributed to the project. The governor gave 1,000 gold coins, 50 bowls, and 530 priestly garments to the treasury. [71] Some of the family heads gave 20,000 gold coins and 2,200 silver minas to the treasury for the project. [72] The rest of the people gave 20,000 gold coins, 2,200 silver minas, and 67 priestly garments.

[73] THE PRIESTS, LEVITES, GATEKEEPERS, TEMPLE SINGERS, SOME OF THE PEOPLE, TEMPLE SERVANTS, AND ALL ISRAEL SETTLED IN THEIR TOWNS.

EXODUS 28:29–30

[29] "Whenever he enters the sanctuary, Aaron is to carry the names of Israel's sons over his heart on the breastpiece for decisions, as a continual reminder before the Lord. [30] Place the Urim and Thummim in the breastpiece for decisions, so that they will also be over Aaron's heart whenever he comes before the Lord. Aaron will continually carry the means of decisions for the Israelites over his heart before the Lord."

PSALM 34:19–22

19 One who is righteous has many adversities,
but the LORD rescues him from them all.
20 He protects all his bones;
not one of them is broken.

21 Evil brings death to the wicked,
and those who hate the righteous will be punished.
22 The Lord redeems the life of his servants,
and all who take refuge in him
will not be punished.

TITLE

THE BOOK OF NEHEMIAH AND THE LIFE OF CHRIST

The book of Nehemiah contains several details that point to the coming work of Jesus. These parallels aren't meant to put Nehemiah on equal footing with Jesus. However, we can learn more about the grand narrative of the Bible when we read the Old Testament through the lens of the person and work of Christ.

Here are several details from the book of Nehemiah that foreshadow the work of Jesus.

THE BOOK OF NEHEMIAH	NEH 2:2-8 Without the walls, Nehemiah knew God's people would never be safe in Jerusalem.	NEH 4:6 Nehemiah rebuilt the walls of Jerusalem.	NEH 2:17-18 Nehemiah's calling to rebuild was the result of prayer and the conviction of the Holy Spirit.	NEH 2:19-20 Before and during Nehemiah's building work, people came to oppose him and tempt him to quit.
PARALLELS	BOTH HAD A MISSION TO ESTABLISH A SAFE PLACE FOR THE PEOPLE OF GOD.	BOTH WERE BUILDERS.	BOTH WERE DEVOTED TO PRAYER AND THE WILL OF GOD.	BOTH WERE TEMPTED TO ABANDON THEIR MISSION.
THE LIFE OF JESUS	Without the resurrection, Jesus knew God's people would never be safe from the power of death. JN 11:25-26	Jesus was a craftsman by trade, but His ultimate building project was the Church. MT 16:18	Jesus' ministry was marked by prayer and submission to the will of the Father. MT 26:36-42	Satan tempted Jesus to abandon the mission of our salvation. MT 4:1-11

NEH 6:1-9 Nehemiah's detractors wanted to physically harm him.	NEH 3 Nehemiah invited other Israelites to build with him.	NEH 1:4 Nehemiah wept at the thought of Jerusalem lying abandoned and exposed.	NEH 13:17-18 Nehemiah cleansed the temple of those who disrespected God's holiness.	NEH 6:15 Though tested, tempted, and opposed, Nehemiah carried out his calling and finished rebuilding Jerusalem's walls .
BOTH HAD ENEMIES WHO PLOTTED TO HARM THEM.	**BOTH CALLED GOD'S PEOPLE TO JOIN THEM IN THEIR WORK.**	**BOTH WEPT OVER JERUSALEM.**	**BOTH CLEANSED THE TEMPLE.**	**BOTH FINISHED THE WORK THEY SET OUT TO DO.**
The religious leaders in Jerusalem plotted to kill Jesus. JN 11:45-54	Jesus calls His followers to participate in building the Church on earth. MT 28:18-20	Jesus wept over Jerusalem's refusal to embrace security in Him. LK 19:41-44	Jesus cleansed the temple of those who sought to turn the temple into a marketplace. JN 2:13-22	Though scorned, beaten, and killed, Jesus finished His work of defeating death by rising from the grave. JN 19:28-30; 20:11-18

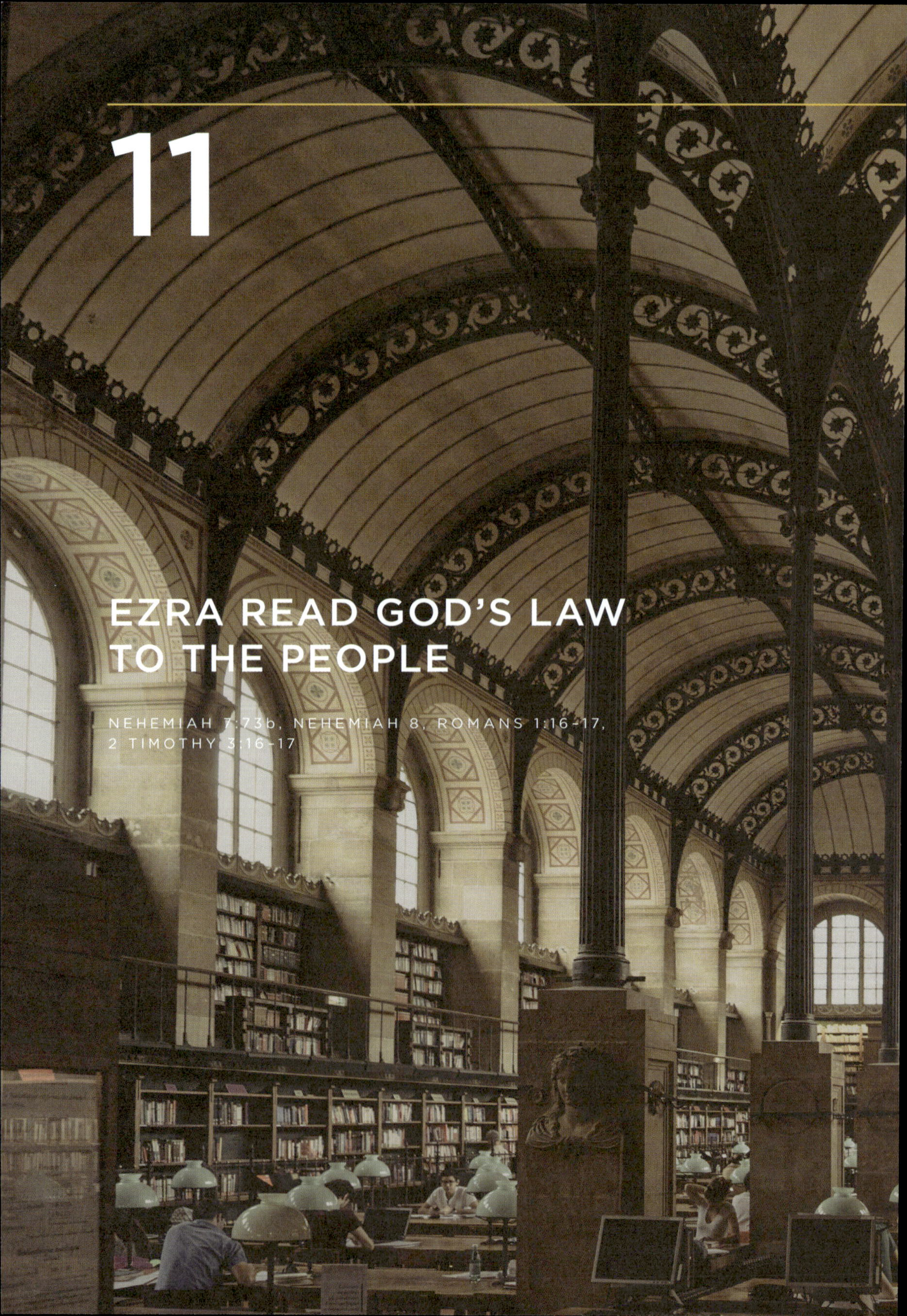

11

EZRA READ GOD'S LAW TO THE PEOPLE

NEHEMIAH 7:73b, NEHEMIAH 8, ROMANS 1:16-17,
2 TIMOTHY 3:16-17

MONTE-CHARGE

NOTES

NEHEMIAH 7:73b

Public Reading of the Law

When the seventh month came and the Israelites had settled in their towns,

NEHEMIAH 8

1 all the people gathered together at the square in front of the Water Gate. They asked the scribe Ezra to bring the book of the law of Moses that the LORD had given Israel. 2 On the first day of the seventh month, the priest Ezra brought the law before the assembly of men, women, and all who could listen with understanding. 3 While he was facing the square in front of the Water Gate, he read out of it from daybreak until noon before the men, the women, and those who could understand. All the people listened attentively to the book of the law. 4 The scribe Ezra stood on a high wooden platform made for this purpose. Mattithiah, Shema, Anaiah, Uriah, Hilkiah, and Maaseiah stood beside him on his right; to his left were Pedaiah, Mishael, Malchijah, Hashum, Hash-baddanah, Zechariah, and Meshullam. 5 Ezra opened the book in full view of all the people, since he was elevated above everyone. As he opened it, all the people stood up. 6 Ezra blessed the LORD, the great God, and with their hands uplifted all the people said, "Amen, Amen!" Then they knelt low and worshiped the LORD with their faces to the ground.

7 Jeshua, Bani, Sherebiah, Jamin, Akkub, Shabbethai, Hodiah, Maaseiah, Kelita, Azariah, Jozabad, Hanan, and Pelaiah, who were Levites, explained the law to the people as they stood in their places. 8 They read out of the book of the law of God, translating and giving the meaning so that the people could understand what was read. 9 Nehemiah the governor, Ezra the priest and scribe, and the Levites who were instructing the people said to all of them, "This day is holy to the LORD your God. Do not mourn or weep." For all the people were weeping as they heard the words of the law. 10 Then he said to them, "Go and eat what is rich, drink what is sweet, and send portions to those who have nothing prepared, since today is holy to our Lord.

DO NOT GRIEVE, BECAUSE THE JOY OF THE LORD IS YOUR STRENGTH."

11 And the Levites quieted all the people, saying, "Be still, since today is holy. Don't grieve." 12 Then all the people began to eat and drink, send

portions, and have a great celebration, because they had understood the words that were explained to them.

NOTES

Festival of Shelters Observed

[13] On the second day, the family heads of all the people, along with the
priests and Levites, assembled before the scribe Ezra to study the words of
the law. [14] They found written in the law how the LORD had commanded
through Moses that the Israelites should dwell in shelters during the
festival of the seventh month. [15] So they proclaimed and spread this news
throughout their towns and in Jerusalem, saying, "Go out to the hill
country and bring back branches of olive, wild olive, myrtle, palm, and
other leafy trees to make shelters, just as it is written." [16] The people
went out, brought back branches, and made shelters for themselves on
each of their rooftops and courtyards, the court of the house of God,
the square by the Water Gate, and the square by the Ephraim Gate.
[17] The whole community that had returned from exile made shelters and
lived in them. The Israelites had not celebrated like this from the days of
Joshua son of Nun until that day. And there was tremendous joy. [18] Ezra
read out of the book of the law of God every day, from the first day to the
last. The Israelites celebrated the festival for seven days, and on the eighth
day there was an assembly, according to the ordinance.

ROMANS 1:16–17

The Righteous Will Live by Faith

[16] FOR I AM NOT ASHAMED OF THE GOSPEL,

because it is the power of God for salvation to everyone who believes,
first to the Jew, and also to the Greek. [17] For in it the righteousness
of God is revealed from faith to faith, just as it is written: The righteous
will live by faith.

2 TIMOTHY 3:16–17

[16] All Scripture is inspired by God and is profitable for teaching, for
rebuking, for correcting, for training in righteousness, [17] so that the man
of God may be complete, equipped for every good work.

12 OUR NATION CONFESSED OUR SIN

NEHEMIAH 9:1-37, 2 CORINTHIANS 1:20-22

NEHEMIAH 9:1–37

National Confession of Sin

[1] On the twenty-fourth day of this month the Israelites assembled; they were fasting,
wearing sackcloth, and had put dust on their heads. [2] Those of Israelite descent
separated themselves from all foreigners, and they stood and confessed their sins
and the iniquities of their fathers. [3] While they stood in their places, they read from
the book of the law of the LORD their God for a fourth of the day and spent another
fourth of the day in confession and worship of the LORD their God. [4] Jeshua, Bani,
Kadmiel, Shebaniah, Bunni, Sherebiah, Bani, and Chenani stood on the raised
platform built for the Levites and cried out loudly to the LORD their God. [5] Then
the Levites—Jeshua, Kadmiel, Bani, Hashabneiah, Sherebiah, Hodiah, Shebaniah,
and Pethahiah—said,

"STAND UP. BLESSED BE THE LORD YOUR GOD FROM EVERLASTING TO EVERLASTING."

Blessed be your glorious name,
and may it be exalted above all blessing and praise.
[6] You, LORD, are the only God.
You created the heavens,
the highest heavens with all their stars,
the earth and all that is on it,
the seas and all that is in them.

NOTES

You give life to all of them,
and all the stars of heaven worship you.
7 You, the LORD,
are the God who chose Abram
and brought him out of Ur of the Chaldeans,
and changed his name to Abraham.
8 You found his heart faithful in your sight,
and made a covenant with him
to give the land of the Canaanites,
Hethites, Amorites, Perizzites,
Jebusites, and Girgashites—
to give it to his descendants.
You have fulfilled your promise,
for you are righteous.

9 You saw the oppression of our ancestors in Egypt
and heard their cry at the Red Sea.
10 You performed signs and wonders against Pharaoh,
all his officials, and all the people of his land,
for you knew how arrogantly they treated our ancestors.
You made a name for yourself
that endures to this day.
11 You divided the sea before them,
and they crossed through it on dry ground.
You hurled their pursuers into the depths
like a stone into raging water.
12 You led them with a pillar of cloud by day,
and with a pillar of fire by night,
to illuminate the way they should go.
13 You came down on Mount Sinai,
and spoke to them from heaven.
You gave them impartial ordinances, reliable instructions,
and good statutes and commands.
14 You revealed your holy Sabbath to them,
and gave them commands, statutes, and instruction
through your servant Moses.
15 You provided bread from heaven for their hunger;
you brought them water from the rock for their thirst.

NOTES

You told them to go in and possess the land
you had sworn to give them.

[16] But our ancestors acted arrogantly;
they became stiff-necked and did not listen to your commands.
[17] They refused to listen
and did not remember your wonders
you performed among them.
They became stiff-necked and appointed a leader
to return to their slavery in Egypt.
But you are a forgiving God,
gracious and compassionate,
slow to anger and abounding in faithful love,
and you did not abandon them.
[18] Even after they had cast an image of a calf
for themselves and said,
"This is your god who brought you out of Egypt,"
and they had committed terrible blasphemies,
[19] you did not abandon them in the wilderness
because of your great compassion.
During the day the pillar of cloud
never turned away from them,
guiding them on their journey.
And during the night the pillar of fire
illuminated the way they should go.
[20] You sent your good Spirit to instruct them.
You did not withhold your manna from their mouths,
and you gave them water for their thirst.
[21] You provided for them in the wilderness forty years,
and they lacked nothing.
Their clothes did not wear out,
and their feet did not swell.

[22] You gave them kingdoms and peoples
and established boundaries for them.
They took possession
of the land of King Sihon of Heshbon
and of the land of King Og of Bashan.

MAPA
MAPA

[23] You multiplied their descendants
like the stars of the sky
and brought them to the land
you told their ancestors to go in and possess.
[24] So their descendants went in and possessed the land:
You subdued the Canaanites who inhabited the land before them
and handed their kings and the surrounding peoples over to them,
to do as they pleased with them.
[25] They captured fortified cities and fertile land
and took possession of well-supplied houses,
cisterns cut out of rock, vineyards,
olive groves, and fruit trees in abundance.
They ate, were filled,
became prosperous, and delighted in your great goodness.

[26] But they were disobedient and rebelled against you.
They flung your law behind their backs

NOTES

and killed your prophets
who warned them
in order to turn them back to you.
They committed terrible blasphemies.
27 So you handed them over to their enemies,
who oppressed them.
In their time of distress, they cried out to you,
and you heard from heaven.
In your abundant compassion
you gave them deliverers, who rescued them
from the power of their enemies.
28 But as soon as they had relief,
they again did what was evil in your sight.
So you abandoned them to the power of their enemies,
who dominated them.
When they cried out to you again,
you heard from heaven and rescued them
many times in your compassion.
29 You warned them to turn back to your law,
but they acted arrogantly
and would not obey your commands.
They sinned against your ordinances,
which a person will live by if he does them.
They stubbornly resisted,
stiffened their necks, and would not obey.
30 You were patient with them for many years,
and your Spirit warned them through your prophets,
but they would not listen.
Therefore, you handed them over to the surrounding peoples.
31 However, in your abundant compassion,
you did not destroy them or abandon them,
for you are a gracious and compassionate God.

32 So now, our God—the great, mighty,
and awe-inspiring God who keeps his gracious covenant—
do not view lightly all the hardships that have afflicted us,
our kings and leaders,
our priests and prophets,

our ancestors and all your people,
from the days of the Assyrian kings until today.
33 You are righteous concerning all that has happened to us,
because you have acted faithfully,
while we have acted wickedly.
34 Our kings, leaders, priests, and ancestors
did not obey your law
or listen to your commands
and warnings you gave them.
35 When they were in their kingdom,
with your abundant goodness that you gave them,
and in the spacious and fertile land you set before them,
they would not serve you or turn from their wicked ways.

36 Here we are today,
slaves in the land you gave our ancestors
so that they could enjoy its fruit and its goodness.
Here we are—slaves in it!
37 Its abundant harvest goes to the kings
you have set over us,
because of our sins.
They rule over our bodies
and our livestock as they please.
We are in great distress.

NOTES

2 CORINTHIANS 1:20–22

20 FOR EVERY ONE OF GOD'S PROMISES IS "YES" IN HIM.

Therefore, through him we also say "Amen" to the glory of God. 21 Now
it is God who strengthens us together with you in Christ, and who has
anointed us. 22 He has also put his seal on us and given us the Spirit in
our hearts as a down payment.

13

GRACE DAY

Use today to pray, rest, and reflect on this week's reading, giving thanks for the grace that is ours in Christ.

FOR I AM NOT ASHAMED OF THE GOSPEL, BECAUSE IT IS THE POWER OF GOD FOR SALVATION TO EVERYONE WHO BELIEVES, FIRST TO THE JEW, AND ALSO TO THE GREEK. FOR IN IT THE RIGHTEOUSNESS OF GOD IS REVEALED FROM FAITH TO FAITH, JUST AS IT IS WRITTEN: THE RIGHTEOUS WILL LIVE BY FAITH.

ROMANS 1:16-17

14

WEEKLY TRUTH

Scripture is God-breathed and true. When we memorize it, we carry the gospel with us wherever we go.

This week's verse is a prayer for continuing to do the work God sets before us.

BUT NOW, MY GOD, STRENGTHEN MY HANDS.

NEHEMIAH 6:9

Find the corresponding memory card in the back of your book.

15

WE PROMISED TO BE FAITHFUL TO GOD

NEHEMIAH 9:38, NEHEMIAH 10, JOHN 14:15, HEBREWS 4:15

NEHEMIAH 9:38

Israel's Vow of Faithfulness

In view of all this, we are making a binding agreement in writing on a sealed document containing the names of our leaders, Levites, and priests.

NEHEMIAH 10

1 Those whose seals were on the document were

the governor Nehemiah son of Hacaliah, and Zedekiah,
2 Seraiah, Azariah, Jeremiah,
3 Pashhur, Amariah, Malchijah,
4 Hattush, Shebaniah, Malluch,
5 Harim, Meremoth, Obadiah,
6 Daniel, Ginnethon, Baruch,
7 Meshullam, Abijah, Mijamin,
8 Maaziah, Bilgai, and Shemaiah.
These were the priests.

9 The Levites were
Jeshua son of Azaniah,
Binnui of the sons of Henadad, Kadmiel,
10 and their brothers
Shebaniah, Hodiah, Kelita, Pelaiah, Hanan,
11 Mica, Rehob, Hashabiah,
12 Zaccur, Sherebiah, Shebaniah,
13 Hodiah, Bani, and Beninu.

14 The heads of the people were
Parosh, Pahath-moab, Elam, Zattu, Bani,
15 Bunni, Azgad, Bebai,
16 Adonijah, Bigvai, Adin,
17 Ater, Hezekiah, Azzur,
18 Hodiah, Hashum, Bezai,
19 Hariph, Anathoth, Nebai,
20 Magpiash, Meshullam, Hezir,
21 Meshezabel, Zadok, Jaddua,

NOTES

[22] Pelatiah, Hanan, Anaiah,
[23] Hoshea, Hananiah, Hasshub,
[24] Hallohesh, Pilha, Shobek,
[25] Rehum, Hashabnah, Maaseiah,
[26] Ahijah, Hanan, Anan,
[27] Malluch, Harim, Baanah.

[28] The rest of the people—the priests, Levites, gatekeepers, singers, and temple servants, along with their wives, sons, and daughters, everyone who is able to understand and who has separated themselves from the surrounding peoples to obey the law of God— [29] join with their noble brothers and commit themselves with a sworn oath to follow the law of God given through God's servant Moses and to obey carefully all the commands, ordinances, and statutes of the LORD our Lord.

Details of the Vow

[30] We will not give our daughters in marriage to the surrounding peoples and will not take their daughters as wives for our sons.

[31] When the surrounding peoples bring merchandise or any kind of grain to sell on the Sabbath day, we will not buy from them on the Sabbath or a holy day. We will also leave the land uncultivated in the seventh year and will cancel every debt.

[32] We will impose the following commands on ourselves:

To give an eighth of an ounce of silver yearly for the service of the house of our God: [33] the bread displayed before the LORD, the daily grain offering, the regular burnt offering, the Sabbath and New Moon offerings, the appointed festivals, the holy things, the sin offerings to atone for Israel, and for all the work of the house of our God.

[34] We have cast lots among the priests, Levites, and people for the donation of wood by our ancestral families at the appointed times each year. They are to bring the wood to our God's house to burn on the altar of the LORD our God, as it is written in the law.

[35] WE WILL BRING THE FIRSTFRUITS OF OUR LAND AND OF EVERY FRUIT TREE TO THE LORD'S HOUSE YEAR BY YEAR.

NOTES

[36] We will also bring the firstborn of our sons and our livestock,
as prescribed by the law, and will bring the firstborn of our herds
and flocks to the house of our God, to the priests who serve in our
God's house. [37] We will bring a loaf from our first batch of dough to
the priests at the storerooms of the house of our God. We will also
bring the firstfruits of our grain offerings, of every fruit tree, and of
the new wine and fresh oil. A tenth of our land's produce belongs
to the Levites, for the Levites are to collect the one-tenth offering in
all our agricultural towns. [38] A priest from Aaron's descendants is to
accompany the Levites when they collect the tenth, and the Levites
are to take a tenth of this offering to the storerooms of the treasury in
the house of our God. [39] For the Israelites and the Levites are to bring
the contributions of grain, new wine, and fresh oil to the storerooms
where the articles of the sanctuary are kept and where the priests
who minister are, along with the gatekeepers and singers. We will not
neglect the house of our God.

JOHN 14:15

"IF YOU LOVE ME, YOU WILL KEEP MY COMMANDS."

HEBREWS 4:15

For we do not have a high priest who is unable to sympathize with our weaknesses, but one who has been tempted in every way as we are, yet without sin.

16

WE RESETTLED JERUSALEM

NEHEMIAH 11:1-21, DEUTERONOMY 7:9,
HEBREWS 11:13-16

NEHEMIAH 11:1–21

Resettling Jerusalem

1 Now the leaders of the people stayed in Jerusalem, and the rest of the
people cast lots for one out of ten to come and live in Jerusalem, the holy
city, while the other nine-tenths remained in their towns. 2 The people
blessed all the men who volunteered to live in Jerusalem.

3 These are the heads of the province who stayed in Jerusalem (but in
the villages of Judah each lived on his own property in their towns—the
Israelites, priests, Levites, temple servants, and descendants of Solomon's
servants— 4 while some of the descendants of Judah and Benjamin
settled in Jerusalem):

Judah's descendants:

Athaiah son of Uzziah, son of Zechariah, son of Amariah, son of
Shephatiah, son of Mahalalel, of Perez's descendants; 5 and Maaseiah
son of Baruch, son of Col-hozeh, son of Hazaiah, son of Adaiah, son
of Joiarib, son of Zechariah, a descendant of the Shilonite. 6 The total
number of Perez's descendants, who settled in Jerusalem, was 468
capable men.

7 These were Benjamin's descendants:

Sallu son of Meshullam, son of Joed, son of Pedaiah, son of Kolaiah,
son of Maaseiah, son of Ithiel, son of Jeshaiah, 8 and after him Gabbai
and Sallai: 928. 9 Joel son of Zichri was the officer over them, and
Judah son of Hassenuah was second in command over the city.

10 The priests:

Jedaiah son of Joiarib, Jachin, and 11 Seraiah son of Hilkiah, son
of Meshullam, son of Zadok, son of Meraioth, son of Ahitub, the
chief official of God's temple, 12 and their relatives who did the work
at the temple: 822. Adaiah son of Jeroham, son of Pelaliah, son of
Amzi, son of Zechariah, son of Pashhur, son of Malchijah 13 and
his relatives, the heads of families: 242. Amashsai son of Azarel, son
of Ahzai, son of Meshillemoth, son of Immer, 14 and their relatives,
capable men: 128. Zabdiel son of Haggedolim, was their chief.

NOTES

[15] The Levites:

Shemaiah son of Hasshub, son of Azrikam, son of Hashabiah, son of Bunni; [16] and Shabbethai and Jozabad, from the heads of the Levites, who supervised the work outside the house of God; [17] Mattaniah son of Mica, son of Zabdi, son of Asaph, the one who began the thanksgiving in prayer; Bakbukiah, second among his relatives; and Abda son of Shammua, son of Galal, son of Jeduthun. [18] All the Levites in the holy city: 284.

[19] The gatekeepers:

Akkub, Talmon, and their relatives, who guarded the city gates: 172.

[20] The rest of Israel, the priests, and the Levites were in all the villages of Judah, each on his own inherited property. [21] The temple servants lived on Ophel; Ziha and Gishpa supervised the temple servants.

DEUTERONOMY 7:9

Know that the LORD your God is God, the faithful God who keeps his gracious covenant loyalty for a thousand generations with those who love him and keep his commands.

HEBREWS 11:13–16

[13] These all died in faith, although they had not received the things that were promised. But they saw them from a distance, greeted them, and confessed that they were foreigners and temporary residents on the earth. [14] Now those who say such things make it clear that they are seeking a homeland. [15] If they were thinking about where they came from, they would have had an opportunity to return.

[16] But they now desire a better place—a heavenly one.

Therefore, God is not ashamed to be called their God, for he has prepared a city for them.

STAND UP AND BLESS THE LORD

TEXT: JAMES MONTGOMERY, 1825

TUNE: AARON WILLIAMS, 1763

1. Stand up and bless the___ Lord you___ peo - ple___ of His choice;
2. O for the li - ving_ flame, from_ God's own_ al - tar brought,
3. God is our strength and___ song, and___ His sal - va - tion ours;
4. Stand up and bless the___ Lord, the___ Lord your_ God a - dore;
stand up and bless the Lord your God with heart and___ soul and voice.
to touch our lips, our minds in - spire, and wing to heaven our thought
then be His love in Christ pro-claimed with all our___ ran - somed powers.
stand up and bless His glo -rious name, both now and___ e - ver - more.

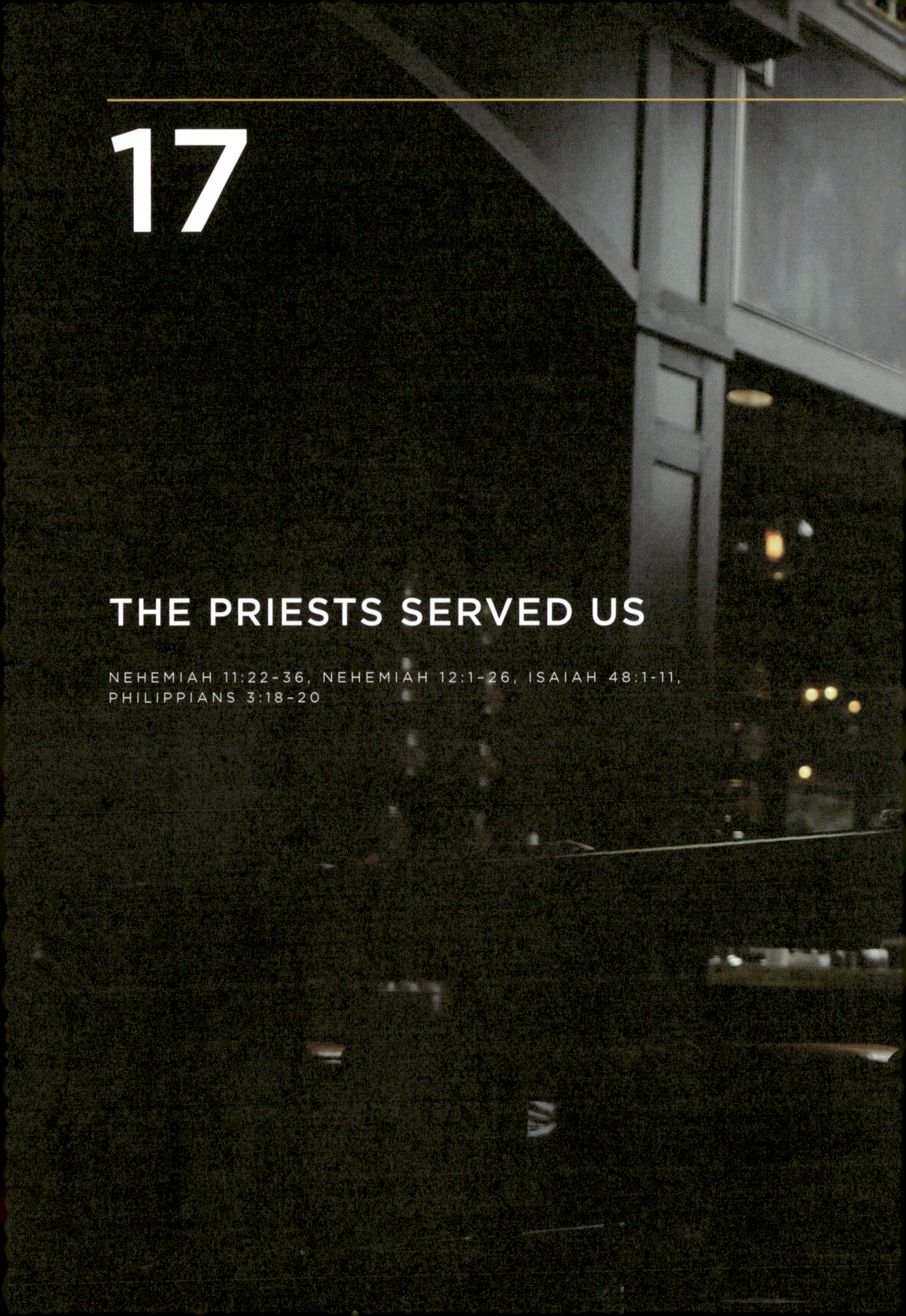

17

THE PRIESTS SERVED US

NEHEMIAH 11:22-36, NEHEMIAH 12:1-26, ISAIAH 48:1-11,
PHILIPPIANS 3:18-20

NOTES

NEHEMIAH 11:22–36

The Levites and Priests

[22] The leader of the Levites in Jerusalem was Uzzi son of Bani, son of
Hashabiah, son of Mattaniah, son of Mica, of the descendants of Asaph,
who were singers for the service of God's house. [23] There was, in fact, a
command of the king regarding them, and an ordinance regulating the
singers' daily tasks. [24] Pethahiah son of Meshezabel, of the descendants
of Zerah son of Judah, was the king's agent in every matter concerning
the people.

[25] As for the farming settlements with their fields:

Some of Judah's descendants lived in Kiriath-arba
and Dibon and their surrounding villages, and Jekabzeel and its
settlements;
[26] in Jeshua, Moladah, Beth-pelet,
[27] Hazar-shual, and Beer-sheba and its surrounding villages;
[28] in Ziklag and Meconah and its surrounding villages;
[29] in En-rimmon, Zorah, Jarmuth, and
[30] Zanoah and Adullam with their settlements;
in Lachish with its fields and Azekah and its surrounding villages.
So they settled from Beer-sheba to Hinnom Valley.

[31] Benjamin's descendants:
from Geba, Michmash, Aija,
and Bethel and its surrounding villages,
[32] Anathoth, Nob, Ananiah,
[33] Hazor, Ramah, Gittaim,
[34] Hadid, Zeboim, Neballat,
[35] Lod, and Ono, in Craftsmen's Valley.
[36] Some of the Judean divisions of Levites were in Benjamin.

NEHEMIAH 12:1–26

[1] These are the priests and Levites who went up with Zerubbabel son
of Shealtiel and with Jeshua:

Seraiah, Jeremiah, Ezra,
2 Amariah, Malluch, Hattush,
3 Shecaniah, Rehum, Meremoth,
4 Iddo, Ginnethoi, Abijah,
5 Mijamin, Maadiah, Bilgah,
6 Shemaiah, Joiarib, Jedaiah,
7 Sallu, Amok, Hilkiah, Jedaiah.

These were the heads of the priests and their relatives in the days of Jeshua.

8 The Levites:

Jeshua, Binnui, Kadmiel,
Sherebiah, Judah, and Mattaniah—
he and his relatives were in charge of the songs of praise.
9 Bakbukiah, Unni, and their relatives stood opposite them in the services.
10 Jeshua fathered Joiakim,
Joiakim fathered Eliashib,
Eliashib fathered Joiada,
11 Joiada fathered Jonathan,
and Jonathan fathered Jaddua.

12 In the days of Joiakim, the heads of the priestly families were

Meraiah	of Seraiah,
Hananiah	of Jeremiah,
13 Meshullam	of Ezra,
Jehohanan	of Amariah,
14 Jonathan	of Malluchi,
Joseph	of Shebaniah,
15 Adna	of Harim,
Helkai	of Meraioth,
16 Zechariah	of Iddo,
Meshullam	of Ginnethon,
17 Zichri	of Abijah,
Piltai	of Moadiah, of Miniamin,
18 Shammua	of Bilgah,
Jehonathan	of Shemaiah,

NOTES

NOTES

19 Mattenai	of Joiarib,
Uzzi	of Jedaiah,
20 Kallai	of Sallai,
Eber	of Amok,
21 Hashabiah	of Hilkiah,
and Nethanel	of Jedaiah.

22 In the days of Eliashib, Joiada, Johanan, and Jaddua, the heads of the
families of the Levites and priests were recorded while Darius the Persian
ruled. 23 Levi's descendants, the family heads, were recorded in the Book
of the Historical Events during the days of Johanan son of Eliashib. 24 The
heads of the Levites—Hashabiah, Sherebiah, and Jeshua son of Kadmiel,
along with their relatives opposite them—gave praise and thanks,
division by division, as David the man of God had prescribed. 25 This
included Mattaniah, Bakbukiah, and Obadiah. Meshullam, Talmon, and
Akkub were gatekeepers who guarded the storerooms at the city gates.
26 These served in the days of Joiakim son of Jeshua, son of Jozadak, and
in the days of Nehemiah the governor and Ezra the priest and scribe.

ISAIAH 48:1–11

Israel Must Leave Babylon

1 "Listen to this, house of Jacob—
those who are called by the name Israel
and have descended from Judah,
who swear by the name of the LORD
and declare the God of Israel,
but not in truth or righteousness.

2 FOR THEY ARE NAMED AFTER
THE HOLY CITY,
AND LEAN ON THE GOD OF ISRAEL;

his name is the LORD of Armies.
3 I declared the past events long ago;
they came out of my mouth; I proclaimed them.
Suddenly I acted, and they occurred.
4 Because I know that you are stubborn,
and your neck is iron

NOTES

and your forehead bronze,
[5] therefore I declared to you long ago.
I announced it to you before it occurred,
so you could not claim, 'My idol caused them;
my carved image and cast idol control them.'
[6] You have heard it. Observe it all.
Will you not acknowledge it?
From now on I will announce new things to you,
hidden things that you have not known.
[7] They have been created now, and not long ago;
you have not heard of them before today,
so you could not claim, 'I already knew them!'
[8] You have never heard; you have never known;
for a long time your ears have not been open.
For I knew that you were very treacherous,
and were known as a rebel from birth.
[9] I will delay my anger for the sake of my name,
and I will restrain myself for your benefit and for my praise,
so that you will not be destroyed.
[10] Look, I have refined you, but not as silver;
I have tested you in the furnace of affliction.
[11] I will act for my own sake, indeed, my own,
for how can I be defiled?
I will not give my glory to another."

PHILIPPIANS 3:18–20

[18] For I have often told you, and now say again with tears, that many live as
enemies of the cross of Christ. [19] Their end is destruction; their god is their
stomach; their glory is in their shame. They are focused on earthly things,

[20] BUT OUR CITIZENSHIP IS IN HEAVEN,

and we eagerly wait for a Savior from there, the Lord Jesus Christ.

18

WE DEDICATED THE WALL

NEHEMIAH 12:27-47, HEBREWS 13:15, REVELATION 19:1-8

NEHEMIAH 12:27–47

Dedication of the Wall

27 At the dedication of the wall of Jerusalem, they sent for the Levites
wherever they lived and brought them to Jerusalem to celebrate the
joyous dedication with thanksgiving and singing accompanied by
cymbals, harps, and lyres. 28 The singers gathered from the region around
Jerusalem, from the settlements of the Netophathites, 29 from Beth-gilgal,
and from the fields of Geba and Azmaveth, for they had built settlements
for themselves around Jerusalem. 30 After the priests and Levites had
purified themselves, they purified the people, the city gates, and the wall.

31 Then I brought the leaders of Judah up on top of the wall, and
I appointed two large processions that gave thanks. One went to the
right on the wall, toward the Dung Gate. 32 Hoshaiah and half the
leaders of Judah followed, 33 along with Azariah, Ezra, Meshullam,
34 Judah, Benjamin, Shemaiah, Jeremiah, 35 and some of the priests' sons
with trumpets, and Zechariah son of Jonathan, son of Shemaiah, son
of Mattaniah, son of Micaiah, son of Zaccur, son of Asaph followed
36 as well as his relatives—Shemaiah, Azarel, Milalai, Gilalai, Maai,
Nethanel, Judah, and Hanani, with the musical instruments of David,
the man of God. Ezra the scribe went in front of them. 37 At the Fountain
Gate they climbed the steps of the city of David on the ascent of the wall
and went above the house of David to the Water Gate on the east.

38 The second thanksgiving procession went to the left, and I followed
it with half the people along the top of the wall, past the Tower of
the Ovens to the Broad Wall, 39 above the Ephraim Gate, and by the
Old Gate, the Fish Gate, the Tower of Hananel, and the Tower of the
Hundred, to the Sheep Gate. They stopped at the Gate of the Guard.
40 The two thanksgiving processions stood in the house of God. So did
I and half of the officials accompanying me, 41 as well as the priests:

Eliakim, Maaseiah, Miniamin,
Micaiah, Elioenai, Zechariah,
and Hananiah, with trumpets;
42 and Maaseiah, Shemaiah, Eleazar,
Uzzi, Jehohanan, Malchijah, Elam, and Ezer.

NOTES

Then the singers sang, with Jezrahiah as the leader. [43] On that day they offered great sacrifices and rejoiced because God had given them great joy. The women and children also celebrated,

AND JERUSALEM'S REJOICING WAS HEARD FAR AWAY.

Support of the Levites' Ministry

[44] On that same day men were placed in charge of the rooms that housed the supplies, contributions, firstfruits, and tenths. The legally required portions for the priests and Levites were gathered from the village fields, because Judah was grateful to the priests and Levites who were serving.
[45] They performed the service of their God and the service of purification, along with the singers and gatekeepers, as David and his son Solomon had prescribed. [46] For long ago, in the days of David and Asaph, there were heads of the singers and songs of praise and thanksgiving to God.
[47] So in the days of Zerubbabel and Nehemiah, all Israel contributed the daily portions for the singers and gatekeepers. They also set aside daily portions for the Levites, and the Levites set aside daily portions for Aaron's descendants.

HEBREWS 13:15

Therefore, through him let us continually offer up to God a sacrifice of praise, that is, the fruit of lips that confess his name.

REVELATION 19:1–8

Celebration in Heaven

[1] After this I heard something like the loud voice of a vast multitude in heaven, saying,

Hallelujah!
Salvation, glory, and power belong to our God,
[2] because his judgments are true and righteous,
because he has judged the notorious prostitute
who corrupted the earth with her sexual immorality;
and he has avenged the blood of his servants
that was on her hands.

[3] A second time they said,

Hallelujah!
Her smoke ascends forever and ever!

[4] Then the twenty-four elders and the four living creatures fell down
and worshiped God, who is seated on the throne, saying,

Amen! Hallelujah!

[5] A voice came from the throne, saying,

PRAISE OUR GOD,
ALL HIS SERVANTS,
AND THE ONES WHO FEAR HIM,
BOTH SMALL AND GREAT!

[6] Then I heard something like the voice of a vast multitude, like the
sound of cascading waters, and like the rumbling of loud thunder, saying,

Hallelujah, because our Lord God, the Almighty,
reigns!
[7] Let us be glad, rejoice, and give him glory,
because the marriage of the Lamb has come,
and his bride has prepared herself.
[8] She was given fine linen to wear, bright and pure.

For the fine linen represents the righteous acts of the saints.

NOTES

19 REMEMBER ME, MY GOD

NEHEMIAH 13, JOHN 14:2-3

NEHEMIAH 13

Nehemiah's Further Reforms

1 At that time the book of Moses was read publicly to the people. The command was
found written in it that no Ammonite or Moabite should ever enter the assembly
of God, 2 because they did not meet the Israelites with food and water. Instead,
they hired Balaam against them to curse them, but our God turned the curse into
a blessing. 3 When they heard the law, they separated all those of mixed descent
from Israel.

4 Now before this, the priest Eliashib had been put in charge of the storerooms
of the house of our God. He was a relative of Tobiah 5 and had prepared a large room
for him where they had previously stored the grain offerings, the frankincense, the
articles, and the tenths of grain, new wine, and fresh oil prescribed for the Levites,
singers, and gatekeepers, along with the contributions for the priests.

6 While all this was happening, I was not in Jerusalem, because I had returned to
King Artaxerxes of Babylon in the thirty-second year of his reign. It was only later
that I asked the king for a leave of absence 7 so I could return to Jerusalem. Then
I discovered the evil that Eliashib had done on behalf of Tobiah by providing him
a room in the courts of God's house. 8 I was greatly displeased and threw all of Tobiah's
household possessions out of the room. 9 I ordered that the rooms be purified, and
I had the articles of the house of God restored there, along with the grain offering
and frankincense. 10 I also found out that because the portions for the Levites had not

been given, each of the Levites and the singers performing the service had
gone back to his own field. 11 Therefore, I rebuked the officials, asking,
"Why has the house of God been neglected?" I gathered the Levites and
singers together and stationed them at their posts. 12 Then all Judah
brought a tenth of the grain, new wine, and fresh oil into the storehouses.
13 I appointed as treasurers over the storehouses the priest Shelemiah, the
scribe Zadok, and Pedaiah of the Levites, with Hanan son of Zaccur, son
of Mattaniah to assist them, because they were considered trustworthy.
They were responsible for the distribution to their colleagues.

NOTES

14 REMEMBER ME FOR THIS, MY GOD, AND DON'T ERASE THE DEEDS OF FAITHFUL LOVE I HAVE DONE FOR THE HOUSE OF MY GOD AND FOR ITS SERVICES.

15 At that time I saw people in Judah treading winepresses on the Sabbath.
They were also bringing in stores of grain and loading them on donkeys,
along with wine, grapes, and figs. All kinds of goods were being brought
to Jerusalem on the Sabbath day. So I warned them against selling food
on that day. 16 The Tyrians living there were importing fish and all kinds
of merchandise and selling them on the Sabbath to the people of Judah
in Jerusalem.

17 I rebuked the nobles of Judah and said to them: "What is this evil
you are doing—profaning the Sabbath day? 18 Didn't your ancestors do
the same, so that our God brought all this disaster on us and on this
city? And now you are rekindling his anger against Israel by profaning
the Sabbath!"

19 When shadows began to fall on the city gates of Jerusalem just before
the Sabbath, I gave orders that the city gates be closed and not opened
until after the Sabbath. I posted some of my men at the gates, so that no
goods could enter during the Sabbath day. 20 Once or twice the merchants
and those who sell all kinds of goods camped outside Jerusalem, 21 but
I warned them, "Why are you camping in front of the wall? If you do it
again, I'll use force against you." After that they did not come again on
the Sabbath. 22 Then I instructed the Levites to purify themselves and
guard the city gates in order to keep the Sabbath day holy.

Remember me for this also, my God, and look on me with compassion according to the abundance of your faithful love.

23 In those days I also saw Jews who had married women from Ashdod,
Ammon, and Moab. 24 Half of their children spoke the language
of Ashdod or the language of one of the other peoples but could not
speak Hebrew. 25 I rebuked them, cursed them, beat some of their men,
and pulled out their hair. I forced them to take an oath before God and
said, "You must not give your daughters in marriage to their sons or
take their daughters as wives for your sons or yourselves! 26 Didn't King
Solomon of Israel sin in matters like this? There was not a king like him
among many nations. He was loved by his God, and God made him king
over all Israel, yet foreign women drew him into sin. 27 Why then should
we hear about you doing all this terrible evil and acting unfaithfully
against our God by marrying foreign women?" 28 Even one of the sons
of Jehoiada, son of the high priest Eliashib, had become a son-in-law
to Sanballat the Horonite. So I drove him away from me.

29 Remember them, my God, for defiling the priesthood as well as the covenant of the priesthood and the Levites.

30 So I purified them from everything foreign and assigned specific duties
to each of the priests and Levites. 31 I also arranged for the donation
of wood at the appointed times and for the firstfruits.

Remember me, my God, with favor.

NOTES

JOHN 14:2–3

2 "In my Father's house are many rooms; if not, I would have told you.
I am going away to prepare a place for you. 3 If I go away and prepare
a place for you, I will come again and take you to myself, so that where
I am you may be also."

20

GRACE DAY

Use today to pray, rest, and reflect on this week's reading, giving thanks for the grace that is ours in Christ.

FOR EVERY ONE OF GOD'S PROMISES IS "YES" IN HIM. THEREFORE, THROUGH HIM WE ALSO SAY "AMEN" TO THE GLORY OF GOD. NOW IT IS GOD WHO STRENGTHENS US TOGETHER WITH YOU IN CHRIST, AND WHO HAS ANOINTED US. HE HAS ALSO PUT HIS SEAL ON US AND GIVEN US THE SPIRIT IN OUR HEARTS AS A DOWN PAYMENT.

2 CORINTHIANS 1:20-22

21

WEEKLY TRUTH

Scripture is God-breathed and true. When we memorize it, we carry the gospel with us wherever we go.

This week's verse is a reminder of God's grace and compassion.

REMEMBER ME FOR THIS ALSO, MY GOD, AND LOOK ON ME WITH COMPASSION ACCORDING TO THE ABUNDANCE OF YOUR FAITHFUL LOVE.

NEHEMIAH 13:22

Find the corresponding memory card in the back of your book.